J 978 C LE   **Child Coll**   13240

Cleveland

High country.

Date Due

MY 13 '8	AR 28 73		
JUN 10 '84	JAN 21 '74		
MAY 11 '8	AR 14 74		
MN 9 '8	JUN 20 2008		
NOV 15 '6			
APR 4 88			
MY 21 '6			
AUG			
JAN 17 7			

Enchantment of America

High Country

THE ROCKY MOUNTAIN AND PLATEAU STATES

Arizona • Colorado • Idaho • Montana
Nevada • New Mexico • Utah • Wyoming

By Libra Jan Cleveland

Illustrated by Tom Dunnington

CHILDRENS PRESS • CHICAGO

Educational Consultant for the
Enchantment of America Series:
Marilyn M. Spore, Laboratory School,
University of Chicago

Regional Consultant for HIGH COUNTRY:
Dr. Myra Ellen Jenkins, Senior Archivist,
New Mexico State Records Center and Archives,
Santa Fe, New Mexico

5-16-63
Library of Congress Catalog Card Number: 62-9070
Copyright, 1962, Childrens Press
Printed in the U.S.A.

Contents

The Land — prehistory to present

Location

There is a wonderful and enchanting land that lies between the plains of the middlewest and the coastal region of the Pacific Ocean and reaches all the way from the cold Canadian border to the desert dryness of Mexican boundaries. This is the rugged and exciting land of Idaho, Montana, Wyoming, Colorado, Utah, Nevada, New Mexico, and Arizona.

8

Formation and Change

This stretch of land is full of the proofs of change. The surface of our earth is changing all the time. You can't see much change from one week to the next, but if you take a longer look—from one million years to another—it's enough to take your breath away.

The fossil shells of sea plants and animals found on the highest mountain peaks, now far above any ocean, show us that this land was once covered by a great sea.

Many layers of sand, shells and mud settled to the bottom of this sea. Year after year, the water and each new layer of sediment pressed down upon the layers beneath. Gradually, sand, shells, and mud became rock.

Then a portion of the land was lifted up to form a shore and coastal plain of the shallow marshy sea that reached from the Gulf of Mexico to the Arctic Ocean. The climate was warm and moist—subtropical. Giant rain forests grew in the swampy marshes and dinosaurs walked the land.

The fossil bones and even whole skeletons of these giant lizards have been preserved in layers of rock, just as the shells of the sea animals that came before them were saved for us to see today. Even the trees of the prehistoric forests became petrified, or turned to stone, and now give evidence of the land before man.

After the time of tropical jungles and swamps, the surface of the land shifted and creased when pressure from within the earth cracked the underlying layers of rock and caused them to slip or "fault." The time of mountain building had begun. Mountain ranges reared their jagged peaks toward the sky. Layers of rock were twisted and turned and even folded over double by the shifting earth.

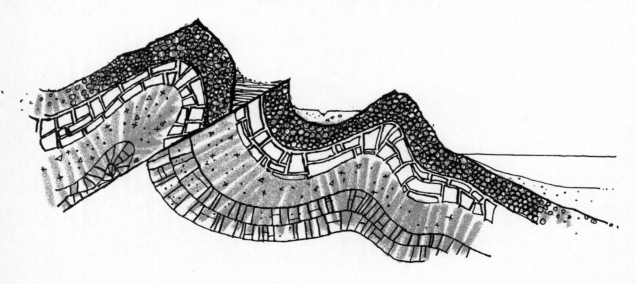

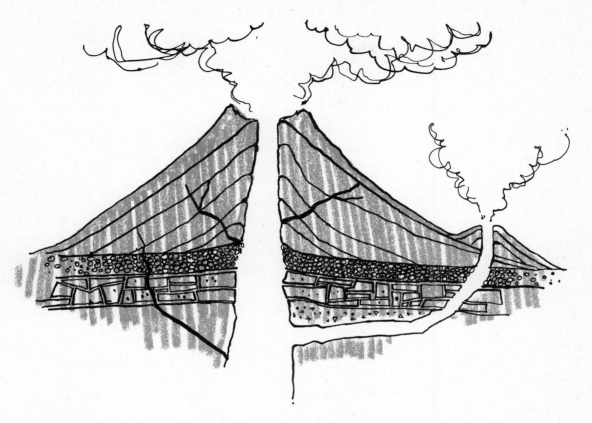

Under tremendous pressure, molten masses of rock from the center of the earth rose through the cracks and faults in the sea-born rocks up to the surface. And the land was lit with the red-orange flames of erupting volcanoes. The air was filled with smoke and flames and ashes. The molten material, white-hot lava, spread over the land, or, built up ever-higher cones around the cracks from which it flowed. New mountains for the land!

The earth settled down. The flames flickered out. The lava slowed in its fiery course, cooled, and then became solid sheets of rock. The climate changed, too. It became cold, and then, warm again.

Monkeys, camels, sabre-toothed tigers and small, three-toed horses took the place of the dinosaurs, gone since the time of the volcanoes and the cold that followed. But jungle animals were not to stay either.

The great Continental ice sheet, born west of the Hudson Bay area in Canada, crept down and covered the land that lay east of the Rocky Mountains. The new mountains, the valleys between them, and the young cascading streams and rivers were silent under their heavy burdens of ice and snow.

When at last the great ice sheet began to recede at the close of the last Ice Age some 25,000 years ago, it filled stream beds with debris, started the Missouri River off to find a new bed, and engraved its calling card with cuts and scars on mountain and canyon walls.

Clouds, heavy with moisture from the Pacific Ocean, hit the mountain wall, then rose higher to cross the rocky barrier. They cooled, and, before they could pass over, dropped their rain. No life-giving rain fell on the far side of the mountains. Beyond the green mountain valleys, the land became dry and barren. The wind swept across the treeless places and took the soil away, leaving slab rocks and sand to keep company with stream-beds, now filled only with boulders. Here were the deserts.

This rugged country of high lands and dry lands, formed in water, flame, and air, began to change as soon as it appeared. Wind, sun, rain, and ice carved and colored its face. These elements of nature, in the process we call erosion, carried away a piece of land there and put it down here; rounded off rough peaks, cut mile-deep canyons, sand-papered plateaus, redirected rivers and made new ones.

Erosion, the slow cutting away and gradual reshaping of the earth's surface, goes on all the time and can be measured in millions of years. But, on rare occasions, a drastic change is made in a few hours.

Only a few years ago, in 1959, strains and stresses built up inside the earth and were released by the faulting of two large blocks of the earth's surface that broke and tilted northward. This was the Hebgen Lake earthquake in southwestern Montana. The force of the quake was felt in eight neighboring states and tilted the bed of the lake so that the north shore was submerged and the south shore raised. Boulders thundered into canyons in landslides. Sections of the earth's surface fifteen miles wide were lifted or lowered.

This earthquake was part of the mountain building that is going on even now in the Madison Range, a group of rugged mountains that are being lifted up from the surface of the earth.

The Lay of the Land Today

The Madison Range is part of the Rocky Mountains, that great range of rugged peaks and high plateaus which extends southeast from Canada through Idaho, Montana and Wyoming, and south through Colorado and New Mexico.

Along the high ridge of the Rocky Mountains is the boundary line between rivers which flow into the Atlantic Ocean and those which flow into the Pacific. This giant watershed, or high land that separates river basins, is the Continental Divide which separates the Atlantic and Pacific drainage systems of North America.

The Missouri, Yellowstone, Platte, Rio Grande and Arkansas rivers flow from the eastern slopes and drain into the Atlantic through the Gulf of Mexico. From the western slopes, the Colorado, Green, and the Snake, which flows into the Columbia, are the rivers that flow to the Pacific from the heights of the Continental Divide.

Spreading across the Continental Divide, a high, dry saddle of land separates the northern ranges of the Rocky Mountains from the Colorado and New Mexico peaks of the southern Rockies. This is the Wyoming Basin.

The Interior Plains to the east of the Rockies, the Great Plains, slope up to the mountains from their beginnings in the low lands of the Mississippi Valley. These Great Plains stretch their western borders of high, treeless, and dry rolling prairies and tablelands over portions of Montana, Wyoming, Colorado and New Mexico.

On the western side of the Rocky Mountains lie the Intermontaine Plateaus where the Snake River cuts the 8,000 foot deep Hells Canyon, North America's deepest gorge, across the dry lava flow lands of the Snake River Plains and the Columbia Plateau to reach the Pacific Ocean.

The Basin and Range Area of the Intermontaine Plateaus is a region of dry valleys that lie between short mountain ranges.

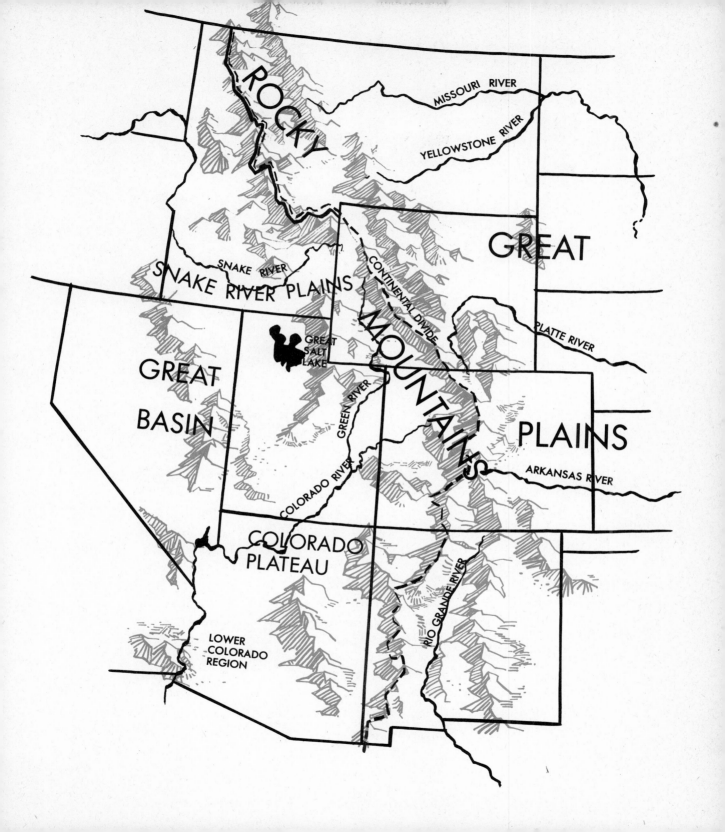

Some of these valleys have no outlet to the sea. The water collects in shallow lakes or low places and evaporates. But the salt and other minerals carried down from the mountains by the water remain. The Great Salt Lake, a lake of this kind in the Great Basin section, is the shrunken remnant of ancient Lake Bonneville whose 50,000 square miles covered the greater part of Utah and parts of Idaho and Nevada during the last ice age.

The Great Basin itself is not really a basin at all but, rather, a plateau region some 4,000 to 5,000 feet high that reaches from southern Oregon through most of Nevada and the western part of Utah. This great desert flatland was built up by soils washed down from the mountains on either side of it—the Wasatch Mountains on the east and the Sierra Nevadas to the west.

The Colorado Plateau, south and east of the Great Basin, is a land of massive uplifts of almost bare rock, bordered by brightly colored

cliffs nearly a mile and half above sea level. The Colorado River and its tributaries have cut and carved deep gorges in the rock layers of these high plateaus. The most famous of these colorful chasms is the Grand Canyon. Over many years, the water's intricate artwork in this region of the Western Highlands produced towering rock pinnacles, natural arches and bridges painted in rainbow hues, and caves with fairy-land formations cut by the rushing waters of underground rivers.

Scattered over the arid sections of this high plateau country are many barren hills. These flat topped hills look like high rock tables rising out of the desert. The Indians call them by the Spanish word for table—*mesa*.

The only real low land in the Rocky Mountain and Plateau region is a small patch in the southwestern corner of Arizona. This area, only about 500 feet above sea level, is the Lower Colorado Region. The land, once covered by the Gulf of California, has been filled in with soil brought by the Colorado River from upstream cliffs and is now a fertile delta.

Climate

The climate of the Western Highlands region is as varied as its land forms. The mountains of this region affect the climate more than any other feature. West winds from the Pacific drop most of their moisture on the western slopes of the Cascade Range and the Sierra Nevada Mountains before they have a chance to reach the high country of the Rocky Mountain and Plateau region. Once on the other side of these great western barriers, the winds pick up any available moisture from the land and its few streams and dry out the country shut in between the Rockies to the east and the Cascades and Sierras to the west.

This land between the mountains is the area of least rainfall in the United States. An average of ten to twenty inches of rain falls on the region each year. But there are desert places which receive no rain at all. Rainfall can vary drastically within the borders of one state, as it does in Utah where some places receive as little as five inches and others as much as forty inches, usually in snow.

The northern part of the Highlands region and the forested mountain slopes receive the most moisture. Here mountain tops are always covered with snow.

Great extremes of temperature, too, exist in this region, depending upon the elevation, the season and the time of day. Mountain temperatures may be extremely cold; deserts have very high temperatures. Yet, at night, a desert may cool off to a temperature of 40 degrees. Summer and winter temperatures of the region vary between a summer mark of 100 degrees and a winter lowpoint of 50 degrees below zero.

This High Country is a land of sunshine since few clouds survive the trip over the mountains and few are formed over the desert and plateau lands.

18

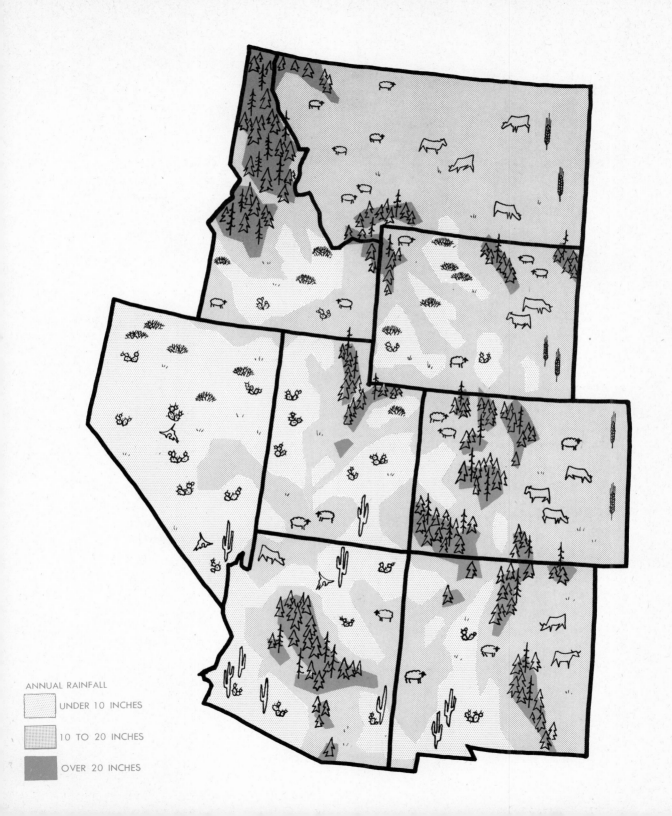

ANNUAL RAINFALL

UNDER 10 INCHES

10 TO 20 INCHES

OVER 20 INCHES

First Men of the High Country

The period of time before written history, before man carved the story of his actions on a stone or pictured them on paper made of reeds, is called *prehistory*. The written history of the High Country did not begin until 1539 when the earliest Spanish explorers set down their accounts of the new land.

But many thousands of years before the Spanish ventured into the land of mountains and plateaus, men roamed the plains hunting herds of big game. Archaeologists call these men the Ancient Hunters. They wandered along the eastern edge of the Rocky Mountains thousands of years before the time of Christ. Even though these people left no written records to tell their story, the carefully made spear points they used to kill the big elephants and giant bison tell us about these first men of the High Country.

The earliest spear points, discovered in the Sandia Mountains, near Albuquerque, New Mexico, date back 25,000 years. The finely-made points of many different shapes used by the Folsom, Eden, Scottsbluff, Plainview and McKean peoples show that these later groups had become masters of stone chipping.

These early bands of wandering hunters were probably composed of a man, his grown sons and their families. They owned nothing that could not be carried on their backs since the movements of the wild herds did not permit them to camp long in any one spot.

In the middle period of High Country prehistory, about 3,000 B.C., the climate of the plains became hot and dry. The grass lands dried up and the herds of giant animals disappeared. Antelope and rabbits, and roots and berries became the main diet of the hunters. Spear points were smaller and not so fine since there was little leisure for artful stone chipping. The people ground seeds on stone slabs to make flour and baked roots in stone-lined pits. They began to raise corn. This was the beginning of the agricultural era and the development of a new southwest culture called the Basketmakers. The people have been given this name because pottery was unknown to them and they used woven baskets for cooking, carrying or storing.

Fifteen hundred years before Columbus discovered the New World, three groups of people lived in the High Country: the Plateau, the Desert and the Mogollon peoples. They lived in shallow caves or pit homes and raised corn and squash. The bow and arrow and houses, as well as pottery, were unknown to them.

First Houses

As time went on and population increased, the art of pottery making was learned and the shallow pit houses in the midst of cornfields came to have roofs.

The climate grew wetter and the bison herds returned to the plains. With the introduction of the bow and arrow, more efficient hunting methods were developed. The Anasazi or "Old People" in the Navajo language, the descendants of the early Basketmakers, retained the basic traits of the bison hunters—the portable tipi, skin clothing and loose social organization. Families hunted alone or in small groups. They came together as a tribe only during the summer when they could be sure of plenty of food.

The people of the plateaus developed an elaborate style of terraced architecture—pueblos—the compact villages, often several stories high, formed by houses joined together around open courts. Pottery took on new forms, colors and uses, and the weaving of cotton cloth began. Here in the High Country, these first thousand years after Christ were years of peace, expansion and progress.

About 1066, the year of the great Norman Conquest of England, Sunset Crater, in the northern part of what is now Arizona, became active. The eruption of the crater covered 800 square miles with a blanket of black volcanic cinder. The area was transformed into a rich agricultural region. News of the good farm land traveled quickly and Indians, particularly from the surrounding desert areas, came to the new farm lands. They planted corn and constructed large pueblos in the canyon walls and cliffs of soft volcanic tuff. An era of prosperity began.

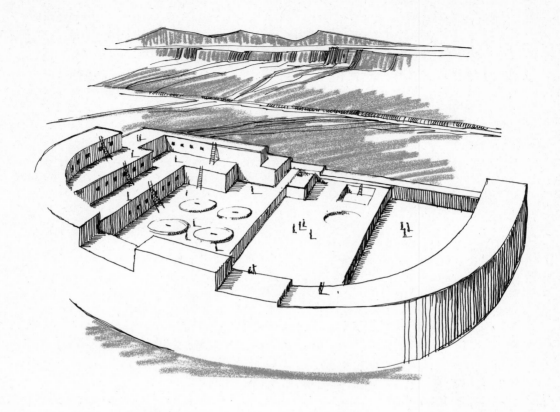

During the twelfth and thirteenth centuries when Christian Europe was marching off to the Crusades, the Great or Classic Pueblo Period marked the height of Pueblo culture. Arts and crafts were at their peak; houses were made of fine horizontal masonry with carefully plastered walls, sometimes decorated with wall paintings and designs. The size of the villages ranged from only a few rooms and a single kiva, or ceremonial room, to the 800 rooms and more than 32 kivas of the Chaco Canyon pueblo which covered three acres. The Chaco Canyon pueblo was the world's largest apartment house until 1847. The people of the pueblos developed an intricate social and political life and a religion of many ceremonies.

Toward the end of this period there was a move from the mesa-top villages to cave and cliff dwellings in canyon walls. The new villages were deliberately fortified. Great towers stood guard over the old Hovenweep hill-top villages in what is now Colorado. Perhaps it was the threat of invasion by wandering tribes that caused these changes.

Another threat to the pueblos came in 1276—the year that saw the beginning of the great drouth which lasted for twenty-four years. Villages were abandoned and, before the end of the drouth, they lay completely deserted as the people drifted south and east in search of water.

In the southern sections of the High Country, in what is now Arizona and New Mexico, the Desert or Hokokam, which means "those who have gone" in the Pima language, and the Mogollon Indians had built many pueblos in canyons and on hill tops. These people devised systems of irrigation canals to carry water from the rivers to the corn, cotton and tobacco fields. After the great drouth, old pueblos were expanded and larger new ones were built to hold the people who came from the north.

Things to think about

How were the different parts of the High Country formed?

In what ways has erosion changed the land?

What causes such differences in climate, some within a hundred mile distance?

What effect did the land and climate have on the first people?

What caused some of the early inhabitants to form communities?

How is it possible to trace the fascinating story of the highland region?

People come to the High Country

Spanish Explorers

After Cortez and the Spanish conquered Mexico in 1519, they heard stories of seven golden cities to the north. In 1536 a Spaniard returned to Mexico City after eight years of wandering to the north. Álvar Núñez Cabeza de Vaca had more stories to tell of the Seven Cities of Cibola.

26

Instead of the seven golden cities there were six Zuñi Indian pueblos in New Mexico. But the gold-greedy Spanish didn't know this.

In 1539 a group of Spaniards, led by Cabeza de Vaca's companion, Estévan, went in search of the Seven Golden Cities. Estévan was killed by the Zuñis and the Spaniards were unsuccessful in their quest for the fabled cities. Despite the Spaniards' futile search for gold, they had been the first white men to enter the territory that is now Arizona.

The following year Fray Marcos de Niza, a Franciscan missionary-priest, accompanied another expedition to the north. This company, headed by Francisco Vásquez de Coronado, conquered the southern-most of the Zuñi pueblos, Hawikuh, and spent the rest of the summer there before moving east to the Rio Grande. It was during this expedition that one of Coronado's captains, Don López de Cárdenas, and his men became the first white men to see the Grand Canyon.

When the Coronado band returned to Mexico, they had not found any cities paved with gold. The next expedition to the north was not until forty years later. Missionaries followed to bring Christian teachings to the Indians and the first Spanish settlement in the High Country was made near the San Juan pueblo in New Mexico in 1598.

On the trail from the Zuñi pueblos of "Cibola" to the Rio Grande was a watering place used by the Indians hundreds of years before the Spanish came that way. Near it stood a huge cliff which the Spanish called El Morro, the bluff. Rising 200 feet above the valley floor, the cliff itself was an impressive landmark and on it the Spanish found hundreds of petroglyphs, markings carved by the Indians long before tales of the Seven Cities brought the Spanish to the bluff.

Two years before the founding of Jamestown, Don Juan de Oñate made the first written inscription on El Morro on his way back to Mexico after discovering the Gulf of California. It read: "Passed by here the Adelantado Don Juan de Oñate, from the discovery of the Sea of the South, the 16th of April 1605."

Later, other inscriptions would be carved in the soft sandstone bluff to be recorded in history.

Spanish Missions and Early Settlement

The early 1600s were the years of the Spanish mission period and early settlement. Santa Fe was founded during the years of 1609-1610, several years before the Pilgrims landed at Plymouth. Missions were built, bringing new crops and improved farming methods to the pueblos that had once been rumored to be golden cities.

The Indians of the Zuñi, Hopi, Salinas, and Gran Quivera pueblos did not take kindly to the Spanish intruders. The priests were tortured and killed. In 1680, all the pueblos rose in revolt.

The Spanish undertook a program of reconquest. Don Diego de Vargas stopped at El Morro and left his name before going to put down the revolt in the pueblos. But the revolt of the Indians and the efforts of the Spaniards at reconquest continued.

28

In the years that followed, Spanish missionaries, soldiers and traders added their names to the Indian petroglyphs on El Morro.

During 1775 and 1776, when the United States of America was just being born, another Spanish priest, Father Escalante, was looking for a direct route to the Monterey Mission in California. These expeditions led him into territory not yet seen by any white man—that of Utah. Father Escalante discovered the immense prehistoric stone houses built of hand carved sandstone blocks in the Las Animas Valley that had housed no less than 1,000 people before the year 1300.

It was Father Escalante, too, who discovered the Green River of Utah. He found many Indians living in the Great Basin region and his reports soon brought many Spanish caravans to the area loaded with goods to trade to the Indians.

French Fur Trappers and Traders

Some two hundred years after Coronado failed to find gold in Colorado, but yet more than thirty years before Father Escalante began to look for a route to Monterey, French fur trappers, looking for the "great river that runs to the sea," came down from Canada, and, on New Year's Day in 1743, were the first white men to see the "shining mountains." The Vérendryes were in the land of the Big Horn Mountains of Montana and Wyoming, looking for the Columbia River. Other French fur traders, pushing west during the early 1700s reached the Colorado country, and in 1739, the Mallet Brothers went as far as Santa Fe.

Lewis and Clark

Except for occasional trappers and a few traders and missionaries, exploration of the High Country came to a standstill. Spain was having troubles of her own after the Thirty Years War, the Wars of the Spanish Succession and bloody civil uprisings. Friction between the Indians and the Spanish in the new world, dissatisfaction with the political power of the church and Spain's economic policy, which drained off the mineral wealth of the Spanish new world, left the country to the north to itself. Mexico prepared for rebellion against Spain.

France, too, had no time to spend exploring the High Country. In 1789, when George Washington became the first president of the United States, France was in turmoil.

Although the thirteen colonies were united under the Constitution and had elected a president to guide them, controversy over the division of power between the state and federal governments prevented any organized effort to see what lay over the mountains.

When Thomas Jefferson became President in 1801, France was engrossed in beginning the end of the general European war that had been calculated to bring the entire Continent under the French flag. It was not difficult to persuade the busy Napoleon to sell French holdings in the West to the United States. The Louisiana Purchase, 1803, added to America's possessions the territory from which all or part of thirteen new states would be carved.

What was all this new land the United States had bought? President Jefferson and America wanted to know. The president urged Congress to authorize an expedition to explore this new country. The party would follow the Missouri River to its source, cross the mountains and reach the Pacific. The Lewis and Clark expedition left St. Louis in the spring of 1804.

During the two years the expedition traveled to the Pacific, and returned once again, Idaho and Montana were mapped and explored for the first time. The Lewis and Clark expedition blazed the trail for other explorers and lit the flame of curiosity in the minds of the people. Scientific expeditions sent by the government soon headed west over the Rockies. Mountain men roamed the valleys and mountains of the new territory in search of valuable beaver pelts. Trading posts were established to buy furs the Indians collected.

Wagons to Santa Fe

After Mexico won its freedom from Spain in 1821, traders, accompanied by heavily laden mules, headed west into the mountain and plateau country to bring goods to the Spanish settlements of the new republic.

The very next year the expedition led by William Becknell opened up a new trail to Santa Fe. Trade was so profitable that soon whole wagon caravans of goods blazed the Santa Fe Trail into the mountains to reach the little mission village that had been built two hundred years before. Santa Fe grew into a prosperous trading center.

Mormons Come Over the Mountains

The great American fur trade was in its last days when the first wagon trains of would-be settlers came over the mountains during the 1830s.

The main advance party of the great Mormon migration entered the Salt Lake Valley late in July, 1847. Soon these early pioneers cleared and irrigated the land, planted crops and built a fort. The very next spring great hordes of crickets descended upon the Mormon settlement. Some of the crops were saved through the efforts of the pioneers with the aid of seagulls which seemed to come from nowhere to destroy the crickets.

Only two years before, in 1846, the lands of Arizona, New Mexico and Southern Colorado had become American property.

Gold

The discovery of gold in California in 1849 sent adventurers and settlers, eager to get rich quick, on their westward way. Towns and trading posts sprang up on the way where the early wagon trains could get supplies.

News of the discovery of gold and silver in Colorado, Nevada, Montana and Idaho during the next ten years started streams of fortune seekers into the High Country. Greenhorns and gamblers, merchants and miners, pilgrims and parasites swarmed in by stagecoach, saddle horse and covered wagon. Stockmen and ranchers who saw a good chance to sell their products to miners settled in the valleys.

The Army came and built forts to protect the people from the Indians who were fighting fiercely to keep their land. Another inscription was made on El Morro. First Lieutenant J. H. Simpson, a part of the Army traveling west, signed his name. An artist who was with him copied many of the older inscriptions to take back east. Soldiers, surveyors and settlers added their names to the rock. In 1857, another signature was added by a Lieutenant E. F. Beale who was the commander of the great caravan of camels sent west to the American deserts.

The Railroad

A gold spike driven at Promontory, Utah, marked the making of the first transcontinental railroad in 1869. New towns sprang up as more people headed west. Lead, zinc, quartz and copper were uncovered and boom towns were built. Opera houses and brownstone or stucco mansions took the place of log cabins. Irrigation systems and the introduction of dry farming techniques made new crops possible. Crops and cattle, ore and wool went east by train. Commercial trade came west.

But it was not until 1886, more than twenty years after the end of the Civil War, and the years of bloodshed and uprisings of Indian Wars, that final peace was made with the Indians and the door opened wide for growth and development in the High Country.

Things to think about

Why did Spanish missionaries and explorers come to the High Country?

How did the Spanish settlements contribute to further development of the region?

How did man deal with the problems that the mountains created?

What present-day customs came from early Spanish influences?

Life in the High Country today

Ranching and Farming

When Coronado and his company first came to the High Country they brought sheep, cattle and hogs for food. The Spaniards who settled later in this region brought sheep and cattle, too. Some of the Spanish cattle escaped and ran wild on the plains. Three hundred years or so later settlers found the descendents of these cattle running wild in small herds. The early homesteaders captured the wild cattle and soon began to raise and sell them. Some settlers brought livestock with them from the East.

In these days of the Old West, there were no fences. The cattle roamed the open range. In the spring cowboys rounded up the herds to brand the new calves so people could tell which ones belonged to whom. In the fall, another round up and the cattle were driven along the trails to the new railroads where they were sent east.

Cattle barons ruled the range during the 1870s and 1880s. There were violent range wars between the cattlemen, and between cattlemen and the sheepmen whose sheep ruined the grazing land for the cattle. Sheep could still thrive where the land was too rough and dry for crops or cattle. Cattlemen and sheepmen fought the farmers who put up barbed-wire fences and fenced off the open range to keep the roaming cattle and sheep out of the fields.

With the aid of the frontier sheriffs, Vigilantes and peace talks, differences were settled—but not always peacefully—and the cattle-men, sheepmen, and farmers set to work to feed and clothe America.

Since the early days of the Old West the production of meat for the nation's tables and wool for the people's clothes has continued to be of great importance in the High Country. Dairy cattle, too, and poultry now come to us from the ranches of the mountain and plateau states.

Although the land of this region has been dry for centuries except for mountain streams, ranching and farming have been important to the people since the prehistoric Indians began to raise corn and cotton. In the desert areas systems of irrigation patterned after the canals of the old Hohokam Indians bring water to the fields, and cotton and grains, fruits and vegetables to the people.

Throughout the High Country, reclamation projects supplement the natural water supply and provide hydro-electric power for homes and industries. Dams collect and store water from rivers and provide year-round supplies of water for many thousands of acres. Some of the biggest dams in the world are here in the High Country. They reclaim land from the desert which would otherwise be wasted.

HOOVER DAM, NEVADA

Mining and Lumbering

The cry of "Gold in the West!" in the middle of the 1800s lured people to the High Country, and the mineral-rich region kept them there. As early as 1863, silver and gold mining in the High Country hit production peaks.

The towns that grew up around the mines or the gold-bearing streams flourished as long as there was gold or silver in the hills. When the minerals were gone, Virginia City, Last Chance Gulch and many other boom towns became ghost towns.

As streams were washed clean, ore veins mined out, and the demands for gold and silver filled, sources of other minerals were discovered.

The discovery of oil in the High Country built more boom towns in the Twenties. Since then, petroleum and natural gas production and distribution have been added to the mineral riches of the region. Uranium, too, that most sought after mineral of recent years, was found in the mountains and canyons of the High Country.

The Spaniards didn't find the gold they were looking for in the early 1500s but miners of the gold rush era, three hundred years later, found the gold and the many other minerals that had lain hidden in the mountains since the High Country was formed. These mountains with their mineral treasures brought the people that built towns in the High Country, and they continue to make this region one of our country's most important sources of minerals for manufacturing and industry. As a result, mining and processing of mineral resources rank among the leading industries in the mountain and plateau states.

Lumber, as an industry in the High Country, varies in economic importance from section to section just as much as the land forms change from mountain peaks to desert plateaus. In the mountainous northern regions where there is more rain, there are more forests. Montana and Idaho claim commercial lumbering among their most important industries. Lumber for many uses comes from the forests of ponderosa pine, fir and spruce trees high on mountain slopes. From these northern areas come many Christmas trees, too. But since a large portion of the timberland of the Rocky Mountain and Plateau states is found at high elevations in hard-to-reach places, there are, for the most part, only small scale lumbering operations.

Much timberland is under government care and control in national forests. Government reforestation and flood control programs carried out in timber areas protect and conserve the forests and the land.

Manufacturing and Processing

Because the Western Highlands region was the last part of our country to be settled, manufacturing and industry were not firmly established here until World War II. In the early days the eastern sections of the country had a head start and the small population and limited markets of the Rocky Mountain and Plateau region made it cheaper to have goods shipped in than to produce them at home.

After 1900, light industries began supplying the needs of the High Country as the population grew and economic activity expanded at a rapid rate. With the coming of World War II, heavy industry made its appearance, helping to supply the whole nation with materials for defense.

Growing interest in and awareness of the security of our country has created a whole new series of industries for the High Country. The electronics industry and the production of missiles involves the manufacture of many, many parts and the installation of testing stations for missiles and nuclear reactors in the High Country.

Manufacturing and processing in the High Country are dependent upon and closely related to mining and agriculture in many ways—for raw materials, and for markets for the products and materials produced.

Natural Resources

Over 200 minerals are found in the High Country. The rich resources of iron, copper and lead ores go into the production of iron and steel which can be used in the manufacture of metal products. When the mineral fuels of gas, coal, and oil are refined the product is power for industry, coke for iron and steel, and chemicals for the manufacture of rubber and plastics.

Forests provide building materials and wood for the manufacture of wood pulp and paper products. Agriculture contributes sugar beets, cattle, sheep, grains, and vegetables to the large food processing industries of the mountain and plateau states. Sugar, beef, flour and bakery goods, canned fruits and vegetables, and potatoes in many forms are the products of these food processing industries.

Water, a very important natural resource in the High Country, is also an important raw material for industry. Huge hydro-electric power plants produce power for industrial use. Dams assure a constant supply of water for the vast irrigation systems of the area. Lakes and streams are the raw materials for the ever-growing tourist industry of the Rocky Mountain and Plateau states.

Transportation and Communication

One of the prime needs of manufacturing and processing industries is transportation. Transportation and communication supply important needs of the community and individual, too. In the old days transportation in the High Country was by foot and horseback; then by wagon and prairie schooner and stage coach.

Pony express riders were the means of communication until telegraph wires reached westward and frontier newspapers printed the news. The first transcontinental railroad tied the East and West together in 1869, only twenty years after the first permanent settlement in Utah. Trains that ran along narrow gauge tracks carried ore down from the mountains.

From the earliest days, and even now, transportation and communication in the Rocky Mountain and Plateau states has its difficulties —the challenge of the terrain. Pipelines carry water and oil and other fuels across the mountains and throughout the areas. Aqueducts and irrigation ditches bring water to desert lands. Trucks carry the raw materials and finished products of agriculture and industry over many miles of highways. Tugboats pull barges loaded with raw materials up and down northern waterways.

Since 1925 when the first commercial air flight was made in the High Country, passengers and many tons of cargo have traveled over the mountains. The motion picture, and radio and television industries bring the Rocky Mountain and Plateau states close to the entire nation. The publishing of newspapers, magazines and books not only brings news and entertainment to the people of the High Country but has become an important industry in itself.

Transportation and communication in all their many phases supply the basic needs of manufacturing and industry by bringing them the raw materials of agriculture and mining and by expanding markets for the sale of finished products. Transportation and communication have contributed extensively to the growth and development of life in the High Country.

The People

The growth and development of a region depends upon natural resources, industry, transportation and communication, and the land itself. But most important of all are people: people to discover, explore and settle the land; people to raise cattle and crops; people to mine the ores and cut the trees; people to turn the natural resources into products that will supply the needs of people. All kinds of people are needed to meet the challenge of the land.

Land and climate influence the kinds and the number of people and the ways they live. The land of the High Country is mountainous; the climate is dry. For many years this region was hard to reach and seemed very far away. Because of these reasons, the Rocky Mountain and Plateau region has fewer people, spread over greater distances, than any other region. The total population of the Rocky Mountain and Plateau states is less than the population of New York City. But the population of this area is growing faster than any other region. City populations are expanding at a rapid rate, sometimes doubling in only a few years.

The people of the High Country are the descendants of the people who built the West. And they are people who still come from the East to the lands of the last frontier.

Some of the people of the High Country are the Spanish whose forefathers made the first settlements and stayed on to see the region grow. The Spanish language and culture are still predominant in many areas of the High Country.

The Gold Rush brought people from all over the world. Immigrants from the old world drifted west from the crowded eastern cities. Irish and Orientals came to build the railroads; English, Scots and Mexicans herded cattle; Basques from the mountains of France and Spain took up their old-world occupation of sheep herding in the new world of the West. Welsh, English and Scots, Poles, Czechs and Slavs worked in the mines; Scandinavians and Finns lumberjacked in the mountain forests; French Canadians came down to trap furs. These peoples came, bringing with them their cultures and their old ways of life to build a new life and a new world in the High Country for themselves and for their descendants who live in the region today. But these peoples were late-comers.

The Indians were in the High Country long before the earliest Spanish explorers came to the region. The detailed way of life developed long ago by the Pueblo Indians remains much the same in the Pueblo villages of today. The Hopi Indian town of Oraibi in Arizona is the oldest continuously occupied city in the entire country. The Hopis, Utes and the Pueblo Indians of the Southwest are settled in the villages of their forefathers. The Apaches are farmers and cattlemen. The Navajos continue to be semi-nomadic, following their herds. But the discovery of uranium, oil and other valuable minerals on Indian reservations has done much to change the lives of some Indians.

Still, for some tribes, life goes on unchanged. The Havasupai Indians live in a village at the bottom of the Grand Canyon, almost completely isolated from the world. The different Pueblo tribes continue to use three completely different and unrelated languages. And the elaborate ceremonials and festivals of the old people continue to be a highlight of Indian life—unchanged except perhaps for the fact that tourists are invited and encouraged to come and watch. The Gallup Intertribal Indian Ceremonial lasts three days and involves some thirty different groups. Each group brings the dances and rituals used by its people long ago. The Navajos continue to weave colorful blankets with skillful artistry and carry on the ancient trade of the silversmith using the symbols and methods handed down for many generations.

The Arts

The culture of the Indians of the Southwest is a substantial part of the High Country's art tradition and heritage. The Indians have long been known for the beauty of their blankets, pottery, jewelry and sand paintings. Their ceremonials incorporate the arts of drama, dance and music. Their adobe dwellings echo the past architectural grandeur of the great pueblos. It is from this culture that many of the arts and crafts of the mountain and plateau states of today have come.

The West and its peoples have furnished exciting and beautiful subjects for stories, poems, paintings and even opera. Bret Hart wrote of the great Gold Rush in *The Luck of Roaring Camp*. *The Ballad of Baby Doe* is a folk opera which tells of silver mines and the people who "struck it rich quick" and lost it just as easily in the early days of Colorado. Mark Twain was full of enough humorous observations about the people and the country, after working on Virginia City's *Territorial Enterprise* in the "Wild West," to write *Roughing It*. The beauties of the highlands and plateaus became poetry in Joaquin Miller's *Songs*. He wrote of the Sierras, the Sunland, and the Desert. Charles M. Russell was a cowboy—and a painter. He recorded the West, its people, and their activities in oils and pencil sketches. Indian stories came from the pen of Oliver La Farge and Charles F. Lummis told of *The Land of Poco Tiempo*. Through ballads of bar-room brawls, paintings and poems of beauty, and piquant reporting, the faraway West was introduced to the rest of the country as early as 1870, and lives on today.

The High Country has developed an art tradition to call its own. A tradition which ranges from the melodramas of yesteryear performed today in thriving "ghost towns" catering to tourists and trading posts offering blankets and jewelry, through the art colony at Taos, New Mexico, begun in 1889 to develop a characteristic Western style. From the famed Mormon Tabernacle Choir in Salt Lake City, the Santa Fe Opera and big city symphony orchestras, libraries and museums, to "Shakespeare Under the Stars" in Colorado and summer theaters in Wyoming where repertory companies perform plays that are old or new.

Architecture reflects the diversity to be found in the arts of the High Country. Throughout the time that the mountain and plateau areas have been inhabited by men, homes ranged from the cliff dwellings of the prehistoric Indians and the pueblos and hogans of today's Indians, through the rough pioneer log houses and turn-of-the-century brownstone mansions, seemingly imported intact from the East, to the modern stone, or adobe and wood ranch houses of today and the designs of tomorrow foreseen by Frank Lloyd Wright and others.

Education

One day in 1859, Mr. O. J. Goodrick pulled his team of oxen to a halt near Cherry Creek. He got out and passed his tall silk hat around the circle of onlookers, collected his salary, and Colorado had its first school. The High Country's mountains and deserts may be full of minerals and romance, and they may be nice to look at, but the distances and the sparseness of the population have, since the earliest days, been a handicap in establishing schools. But now there are school buses, and much of the population has become concentrated in the cities so that there are better facilities for education than the first teachers of the High Country, who traveled by horseback between the small, scattered communities, and the small, mudroofed schoolrooms like Mr. Goodrick's, could offer.

The High Country can boast of many kinds of fine educational centers, some supported by the United States Government—such as the Air Force Academy near Colorado Springs, others by the state, or by private funds. There are public, private, parochial and sectarian schools. There are grade schools, high schools, colleges, junior colleges, universities, technical and training schools, schools for Indians and schools for advanced research and experimentation.

The Kitt Peak, Lowell, and High Altitude Observatories carry on studies in solar radiation and other research important to the fast approaching space age. The peaceful uses of atomic power are being studied at Los Alamos. Special studies conducted in the High Country in aerodynamics at the Air Force Academy and research projects using cyclotrons and nuclear reactors, as well as the testing of missiles and the powers of nuclear energy, are important to our nation's and the world's progress into tomorrow. Agricultural experimentation provides information and new sources of supply for improved food, plant and timber production. Not only is education in the High Country shooting for the stars of a better tomorrow but also for the best possible life today.

In the very few years since man came over the mountains to the deserts, plains, and plateaus of the High Country, many peoples contributed to the development of the region in many ways. Today, people see it grow and expand at a tremendous rate in resources and industrial development, and intellectual activity. Man has used the resources of this land and his own inner resources to meet the challenge of the mountains and plateaus to carve out a home in the highlands.

Things to think about

Why is ranching and farming a big business in the High Country?

In what ways do natural resources contribute to the industrial and economic growth of this region?

How has the expansion of transportation and communication met the needs of industry and manufacturing?

Why is the High Country still one of the least populated sections of the United States?

What are some of the cultural contributions of the highland region?

How does this region provide opportunities for scientific progress?

Everlasting enchantment

Enchantment Waits in the High Country

There are many things to see and do in the High Country. You can climb up a mountain road thousands of feet into the air. You can follow a winding trail thousands of feet below the surface of the earth down into a cave that glitters with lacy spindle formations. You can skate on an icy mountain lake in the middle of summer or get a sun tan while you water ski on warm southwestern waters in the middle of winter.

The Yesterday Corner of the High Country

Dotted over the deserts, clinging to mountain slopes or tucked away in forgotten valleys are the ghost towns. Their names tell many stories—funny and sad, of beginnings and ends—Tincup, Bonanza, Midas and Treasure Hill, Bull Frog and Rabbit Hole.

Some are completely deserted, except for a few bats that listen to the wind swing through creaky shutters and doors. Some—not quite gone to the ghosts—contain a few people who still work the old mines, while others are very lively ghost towns, rebuilt and refurnished to the heights of their Wild West or Victorian glory.

Local pageants and rodeos, too, show the visitor what the West was like in the old days. Frontier Days celebrations all over the High Country call for the costumes and beards of a century ago.

Rodeo is a Spanish word which means a "going round." In the early days of the West, this meant a cattle round up. Now, rodeo means an exciting, festive occasion when cowboys, real or professional, show their skill in calf roping, bulldogging and other activities of the round up. Every day during the summer, there is a rodeo someplace in the High Country.

No matter what the season, there always seems to be an occasion for Spanish fiestas or ceremonial Indian dances. In spring, the Blessing of the Fields and the Spring Corn Dances; then, after the first frost, harvest festivals and celebrations. Christmas Eve in many places means little bonfires in the streets, candle light processions and, in the pueblos, special dances after Midnight Mass.

49

High Country Wildlife

The High Country teems with wildlife.

The hunter, fisherman, camera bug and the just plain curious have an abundant supply of game from which to choose their quarry.

The world's largest fresh water fish, the sturgeon, can be found in the cold mountain lakes of the mountain and plateau states. Streams and rivers hold many varieties of trout and pan fish. Wild turkeys, pheasants, grouse, quail and partridges flock on hillsides and in flatland fields. Ducks and geese choose mountain lakes and rivers while the wily roadrunner speeds along the desert sands.

In the High Country, big game is really BIG game. Bears—black, brown, and grizzly—moose, deer, elk and antelope occupy highland homes along with mountain goats, sheep and mountain lions. And, of course, the West wouldn't be the "Wild" West without the coyotes to howl and the jackrabbits to jump, as well as the little prairie dogs and the rather socially unacceptable horned toads, Gila monsters and rattlesnakes.

The last buffalo, or American bison, herd in existence can be seen here in the High Country. These truly American animals were all but shot out of existence until the Department of the Interior set aside land for their personal grazing range. Other game preserves and sanctuaries in the Rocky Mountain and Plateau states give refuge and protection to animals and birds so that they may survive and we may continue to enjoy them. State and federal Conservation Departments maintain fish hatcheries to stock lakes and streams so fishermen will not be disappointed. They promote the wise use and protection of land, water, plants and wildlife.

National Parks and Natural Monuments of the High Country

Not only can we enjoy the beauty of our land, but we can learn from the land. It holds many stories of our American heritage. The Department of the Interior set aside portions of the land that contained especially interesting or beautiful chapters of that heritage. These are our national parks and monuments. "The National Park System is dedicated to conserving the scenic, scientific, and historic heritage of the United States for the benefit and enjoyment of its people."

Some of the most wonderful and exciting things to see and do in the whole United States can be found in the High Country's areas of the National Park System. Familiar outdoor activities such as horseback riding, hiking, swimming and boating, or nature walks become extraordinary experiences, not soon to be forgotten when your chosen territory touches any of the many wonders of the High Country world.

Enchantment waits for you in miles-high mountains and glacier-filled valleys, monuments to the long ago, and in carved and colorful caves and canyons. There are shifting sands and painted deserts, volcanic regions—new and old—where cones and craters pockmark the surface to create a *moonscape*. Whole valleys bubble with hot springs and blue sky is pricked by spouting geysers that seem to have built-in alarm clocks.

Mountain and Glacier Parks

High among the rugged peaks in the northern region, Glacier, Grand Teton and Rocky Mountain National Parks enclose the magnificent scenery carved and sculptured long ago by glaciers and ice sheets. Alpine wilderness, lush forests on jagged mountain sides, icy glacier-hewn lakes, streams and waterfalls, and ancient glaciers that inch their way up and down canyons and valleys are the landmarks of these three parks.

Glacier National Park, in northwestern Montana on the International Border, is part of the Waterton-Glacier International Peace Park. Grand Teton National Park in western Wyoming surrounds the most spectacular portion of the Grand Teton Mountain Range. Rocky Mountain National Park in the midst of Colorado is high in the Front Range of the great Rocky Mountains. In the park are 65 named peaks between 10,000 and 14,256 feet above sea level, part of the rocky backbone of the nation. Along this backbone runs the Continental Divide.

Monuments to the Long Ago

Mesa Verde National Park on the sunset side of the Rockies in southern Colorado and Dinosaur and Petrified Forest National Nature Monuments are High Country tributes to long ago. Dinosaur, stretched between the northern corners of Colorado and Utah, is a semi-arid wilderness plateau, cut through with deep gorges filled with calm water and the white water of rapids. The exposed, tilted rock layers represent millions of years of geologic processes. Embedded in these layers are the skeletal remains of prehistoric reptiles.

Mesa Verde National Park contains hundreds of prehistoric ruins, once lived in by the ancient Indians. Here you can see the earliest dwellings, the pit houses, as well as the surface pueblos and the later magnificent cliff dwellings. There are many prehistoric villages of the High Country's first people scattered through the mountains and plateaus. These dwellings, preserved over the ages, are now protected and honored as national archaeological monuments.

Arizona's Petrified Forest is a fascinating natural exhibit of sections and even whole trees that fell to the desert floor thousands of years ago. Over many years, the trees slowly turned to stone as minerals replaced the vegetable materials. Ancient Indian ruins and prehistoric Indian markings, or petroglyphs are also within this national monument.

Parks of Canyons and Gorges

Deep canyons, cut wide or narrow by rivers over thousands of years, expose colorful pages of geologic history. The Canyon of the Virgin River in Utah's Zion National Park is the best example of a deep, vertically walled, colored chasm that is accessible. Perhaps the world's most colorful and unique forms of erosion can be seen in Utah's Bryce Canyon National Park. Intricately carved and colored pinnacles, walls and spires rise from the canyon floor.

The grand-daddy of all the canyons was cut across a high Arizona plateau by the Colorado River's carving powers, at work for thousands of years. This canyon is now the central point of interest for one of the most famous national parks. Tinted with rainbow colors, the mile-deep Grand Canyon of the Colorado is one of the Seven Wonders of the World.

Cave Displays

A mile or so under the surface of the earth, spreading outward for many miles, lie the largest underground chambers ever discovered. New Mexico's Carlsbad Caverns National Park is made up of a fantastic series of connected caverns that were dissolved and hollowed out of limestone by underground waters. Lovely, spectacular and weird mineral deposit formations hang down from the ceiling—stalactites—and grow up from the cavern floors—stalagmites.

Both active and dormant phases of cavern development can be seen in Utah's Timpanagos Cave National Monument. Timpanagos is especially noted for its unusual helictites, delicately twisted spiral formations. Lehman Caves, in Nevada, are honeycombed with many tunnels and galleries. The caverns of light grey or white limestone are decorated with massive stalactites and stalagmites and the unique "palette" cave formation.

Desert Monuments

National monuments in dry, desert wastelands hold beauty and enchantment. The Great Sand Dunes in Colorado are among the largest and highest in the country. New Mexico's White Sands monument is composed of glistening white gypsum sand dunes continually piled and shifted by the wind. The desert creatures of this area have become adapted to their environment and are white, or very light in color.

Death Valley, long told of in Western lore, is a vast desert solitude which reaches from the western edge of Nevada into California. Here are the weird natural phenomena of great salt beds and borax formations. Here too, not far from towering mountains, is the lowest point in the Western Hemisphere—282 feet below sea level.

The desert is full of strange things. Among them, the giant cactus forests of Organ Pipe Cactus and Saguaro National Monuments. Here, desert plants found nowhere else trace the old Spanish route, *Camino del Diablo*.

Volcanic Monuments

Capulin Mountain and Sunset Crater National Monuments in New Mexico and Arizona are of special interest because they were volcanoes born very recently, geologically speaking. Cone-shaped Capulin Mountain is covered now with grass, but Sunset Crater remains a symmetrical cinder cone surrounded by lava and ash lands. Wyoming's Devil's Tower is evidence of volcanic activity millions of years ago. This 865 foot tower of column-structured rock was made America's first national monument.

You could easily think you were looking at the surface of the moon through a telescope when you see Idaho's Craters of the Moon National Monument. The surface of this strange volcanic field is scarred and marked by fissure eruptions, cinder cones, craters, and lava flows with weird hollows and caves.

Thermal Park—Yellowstone

Yellowstone, the oldest of our national parks, lies within the borders of three states; Idaho, Montana and Wyoming. The park contains one of the world's largest and most spectacular thermal, or hot water areas.

Yellowstone is a wonderland of great wilderness regions, wild life, rugged mountains, lakes, waterfalls and the great canyon of the Yellowstone River. Disturbances and pressures beneath the park are responsible for some 3,000 geysers and bubbling hot springs. Layers upon layers of colorful mineral deposits have built up around the sources of these strange and beautiful hot-water wonders.

Things to think about

Why have areas of the High Country been preserved as national parks and monuments?

Why are some plants and wildlife found only in this region?

What natural phenomena can be found or seen in this unusual region?

What are some of the things that make this an especially enchanted area of everlasting beauty?

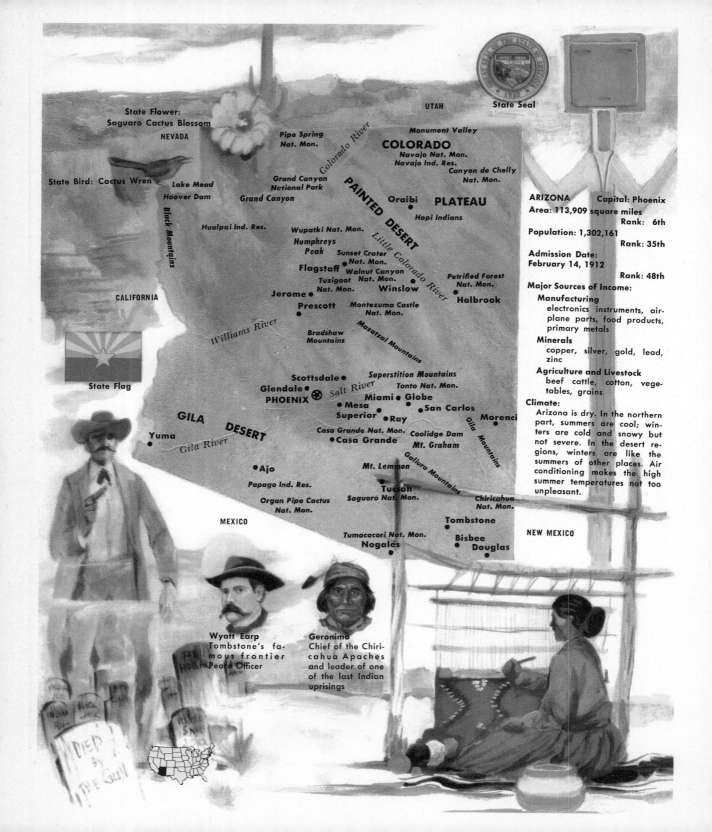

State Flower:
Saguaro Cactus Blossom

State Seal

State Bird: Cactus Wren

NEVADA

UTAH

Monument Valley

Pipe Spring
Nat. Mon.

COLORADO

Colorado River

Navajo Nat. Mon.
Navajo Ind. Res.

Canyon de Chelly
Nat. Mon.

Lake Mead
Hoover Dam

Grand Canyon
National Park

Grand Canyon

Oraibi

PLATEAU

PAINTED DESERT

Hopi Indians

Hualpai Ind. Res.

Wupatki Nat. Mon.

Little Colorado River

Humphreys
Peak

Sunset Crater
Nat. Mon.

Petrified Forest
Nat. Mon.

CALIFORNIA

Flagstaff

Tuzigoot
Nat. Mon.

Walnut Canyon
Nat. Mon.

Winslow

Holbrook

Jerome

Prescott

Montezuma Castle
Nat. Mon.

Williams River

Bradshaw
Mountains

Mazatzal Mountains

ARIZONA   Capital: Phoenix
Area: 113,909 square miles
                           Rank: 6th
Population: 1,302,161
                           Rank: 35th
Admission Date:
February 14, 1912
                           Rank: 48th

Major Sources of Income:
  Manufacturing
    electronics instruments, air-
    plane parts, food products,
    primary metals
  Minerals
    copper, silver, gold, lead,
    zinc
  Agriculture and Livestock
    beef cattle, cotton, vege-
    tables, grains

Climate:
  Arizona is dry. In the northern
  part, summers are cool; winters are cold and snowy but
  not severe. In the desert regions, winters are like the
  summers of other places. Air
  conditioning makes the high
  summer temperatures not too
  unpleasant.

State Flag

Black Mountains

Scottsdale

Superstition Mountains

Glendale

Salt River

Tonto Nat. Mon.

PHOENIX

Miami

Globe

Mesa

San Carlos

GILA

DESERT

Superior

Ray

Morenci

Yuma

Gila River

Casa Grande Nat. Mon.

Casa Grande

Coolidge Dam

Mt. Graham

Gila Mountains

Ajo

Papago Ind. Res.

Mt. Lemmon

Galiuro Mountains

Organ Pipe Cactus
Nat. Mon.

Tucson
Saguaro Nat. Mon.

Chiricahua
Nat. Mon.

MEXICO

Tumacacori Nat. Mon.
Nogales

Tombstone

Bisbee
Douglas

NEW MEXICO

Wyatt Earp
Tombstone's fa-
mous frontier
Peace Officer

Geronimo
Chief of the Chiri-
cahua Apaches
and leader of one
of the last Indian
uprisings

Arizona is a state of many carved and colorful corners. Rough-hewn, barren mountains rise abruptly from the desert floor of the southwest corner. A "Wonderland of Rocks," and rolling hills mottled with sparse vegetation lie to the east. Cool green mountains and valleys curve northward from the eastern border, through the center of the state. In the northeast corner, there is a desert-like plateau, once part of a vast forest that was buried for many years beneath volcanic ash, water, sand and mud. The trees that were buried turned to stone, and now, uncovered, are Arizona's Petrified Forest.

Important Whens and Whats in the Making of Arizona

1539 A group of Spaniards, led by Estévan, are the first white men to enter what is now Arizona.

1540 Francisco Vásquez de Coronado's company, with Fray Marcos de Niza, enters the Arizona region.

1691 Padre Eusebio Francisco Kino begins his work of establishing missions.

1735 The first permanent settlement is made at Tucson.

1737 The Spanish find silver near the Mexican border.

1821 Mexico receives her independence from Spain, and Arizona comes under Mexican rule.

1848 War with Mexico ends and the land north of the Gila River becomes United States property.

1853 The Gadsden Purchase gives the United States the southern Arizona region.

1861-1886 Apache warfare troubles the region until the surrender of Geronimo.

1863 Arizona becomes a separate United States Territory.

1912 Arizona is admitted to the Union as the 48th State.

Strange rock formations and canyons with equally strange names —Spider Web Arch, Monument Valley, Totem Pole—carved from the plateau further north, are Navajo and Hopi Indian territory. Thirteen Indian tribes live in Arizona in pueblos of their ancestors, on reservations, and at the very bottom of the Grand Canyon. The largest reservation in America is home to Arizona's Navajo Indians.

Arizona is rich in oil, minerals and scenic wealth. Almost half of all the copper used in America comes from Arizona mines. Arizona is rich in legends and monuments of the past. Prehistoric Indian ruins, and trails followed by Coronado and his explorers, and by early American pioneers are well-worn footpaths of the past. Yuma Territorial Prison, the last home of many infamous Western desperados, ghost towns and the ghost tale of the Lost Dutchman Gold Mine, which legend says is hidden away somewhere in the Superstition Mountains, pay tribute to Arizona's days of growing up.

And Arizona is full of the signposts of today. Mighty Roosevelt Dam provides power and water for irrigation and recreation. Great fields of cotton, vegetables and grains grow in desert areas where only cactus and prickly pear grew before man brought water from the rivers to irrigate his crops. Cattle graze on the state's vast open ranges, keeping company with prairie dogs, coyotes and jack rabbits.

Electronics and airplane parts manufacturing plants shine in the land of the Cochise Men who lived here 20,000 years ago. Space, atomic and electronic research go forward on mountain peaks, in deserts and canyons that were formed millions of years before man.

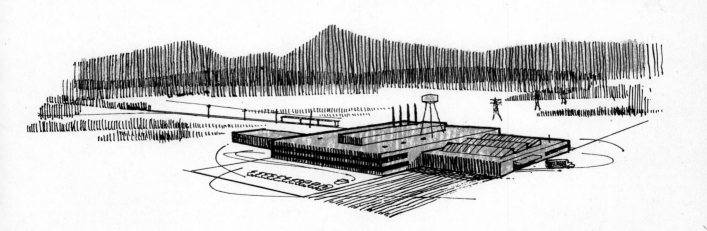

State Bird: Lark Bunting

State Flower:
Rocky Mountain Columbine

State Flag

WYOMING

Dinosaur
Nat. Mon.

North Park
Rocky Mountain
National Park
Estes Park

Steamboat
Springs

Fort Collins
Loveland

Greeley

Sterling

NEBRASKA

Front Range

High Plains

ROCKY

Continental

Longmont

South Platte River

Longs Peak

Park Range

Hot Sulphur
Springs

Boulder

Central City

Golden

Colorado River

Lookout
Mountain

DENVER

Idaho
Springs

Englewood

GREAT

UTAH

Glenwood Springs

Mt. Evans

Aspen

Mt. Elbert

Fairplay

Colorado
Nat. Mon.

Grand Junction

Grand Mesa

Divide

South Park

PLAINS

Gunnison

Pikes Peak

MOUNTAINS

Black Canyon
of the
Gunnison

River

Colorado Springs

Cripple Creek

Royal Gorge

Pueblo

Lake City

Arkansas River

San Juan Range

Telluride

Sangre de Cristo Range

COLORADO

Great Sand Dunes
Nat. Mon.

KANSAS

Hovenweep
Nat. Mon.

PLATEAU

Rio Grande

San Luis Valley

Cortez

Durango

Conejos

River

Trinidad

Mesa Verde
National Park

NEW MEXICO

OKLAHOMA

Zebulon M. Pike
Early soldier-ex-
plorer of the Colo-
rado region and
discoverer of Pikes
Peak

Jack Dempsey
U.S. Heavyweight
boxing champion,
1919-1926

State Seal

COLORADO

Capital: Denver

Area: 104,247 square miles	Rank: 8th
Population: 1,753,947	Rank: 33rd
Admission Date: August 1, 1876	Rank: 38th

Major Sources of Income:

Manufacturing
food products, electronics instruments, transportation equipment, machinery

Minerals
oil and natural gas, uranium, molybdenum, vanadium and zinc

Agriculture and Livestock
beef cattle, wheat and hay, sugar beets, corn

Climate:
Colorado is the highest state in average elevation. Humidity is very low, so winter and summer temperatures are not unpleasant. Mountain ranges protect Colorado from temperature extremes and assure an adequate water supply. The Chinook, a warm, dry wind, is a curious Colorado weather feature which results when cold air from the north is heated and dried as it comes over the mountains.

The state of Colorado is larger than the states of New York, New Jersey and Pennsylvania combined. Within Colorado's borders are three main land areas.

In the east, the High Plains rise gradually from the low, rolling Great Plains to heights of 6,000 feet as they approach the Rockies. The Rocky Mountains, a series of discontinuous ranges, run through the central portion of the state to include the San Juan Range, a tangled core of mountains in the southwest. The Colorado Plateau to the west is composed of different materials than the Rockies. The plateau is cut so deeply by the Colorado River and its tributaries, and so much of the plateau is 10,000 feet and higher, that it is often considered an extension of the Rockies.

Important Whens and Whats in the Making of Colorado

1694	General Don Diego de Vargas enters San Luis Valley with the first white expedition on record.
1803	The northeastern Colorado region becomes the property of the United States through the Louisiana Purchase.
1806	Captain Zebulon Pike makes the first real exploration of the Colorado region from the east.
1833	Bent's Fort is established on the Santa Fe trail for fur trading.
1848-1850	After the Mexican War, remaining Colorado land comes to the United States from Mexico.
1851-1852	Colorado's first permanent settlements are made at San Luis and Conejos in the San Luis Valley.
1858-1859	Discovery of gold in Colorado is followed by the Pike's Peak Gold Rush.
1875-1879	Silver boom.
1876	Colorado is admitted to the Union as the 38th State.

Fifty-five of the seventy-one peaks over 14,000 feet outside of Alaska, are in Colorado. Mount Elbert, at 14,431 feet, is only 64 feet shorter than California's Mount Whitney. Scattered through Colorado's mountains are large basins, high valleys or "parks" where mountain waters collect and then flow into the rivers.

The San Luis Valley in southern Colorado is a "park," enclosed within the mountains and well irrigated by mountain waters on their way to the Rio Grande. Here, in this sheltered basin, San Luis, considered to be Colorado's first town, was founded in 1851. Conejos was settled by the Americans in 1852. Colorado was one of the earliest inhabited areas on the North American continent. Twenty-five thousand years ago prehistoric men hunted huge mammoths and other big animals along the eastern edge of the Rockies. Later Indians built pueblos, some of which can be seen today in Hovenweep and Yucca House National Monuments.

Utes, Cheyennes and Arapahoes roamed Colorado's plains and plateaus, and harassed the early pioneers and settlers who traveled the Overland and Santa Fe trails to the West. Colorado's mountain storehouses contain some 250 known minerals and it was Colorado's gold and silver, lead and zinc that first brought people to the region.

Mining villages, and lumber camps grew up on the mountains and now these early Colorado landmarks have modern winter resorts for neighbors. Thousand-acre farms and ranches with wheat fields and grazing land for beef cattle are spread over the High Plains. The wider and lower Colorado Valley, in the western part of the Colorado Plateau, is famous for its peaches and other fruit. On the other side of the mountains, in the South Platte Valley, Colorado produces more sugar beets than any other state except California.

Skiing and other winter sports are big business in Colorado, especially in sky-high Aspen. Originally a gold town, Aspen is now also widely known for its music festivals. Rodeos, Horse and Livestock Expositions, Grand Opera at Central City, exhibits at Colorado Springs Fine Arts Center and bubbling hot springs at Steamboat Springs are all part of Colorado's colorful charm.

Colorado roads can take you many places. The highest car road on the continent winds its way 14,264 feet up lofty Mount Evans. Highways lead to Rocky Mountain and Mesa Verde National Park or take you into the past to national monuments of long-gone dinosaurs, prehistoric Indian villages, and nature's old and artful ways with rock, water and sand. "Classified" and "Top Security" roads lead to the research laboratories and missile testing grounds of the space age.

State Seal

State Flag

State Bird:
Mountain Bluebird

State Flower: Syringa

CANADA

Sandpoint

Pend Oreille Lake

Coeur d'Alene

Coeur d'Alene Mountains

Cataldo Mission

ROCKY

MONTANA

WASHINGTON

Moscow

Orofino

Lewiston

Clearwater River

Bitterroot Range

Hell's Canyon

Clearwater Mountains

Salmon River

MOUNTAINS

Salmon River Mountains

Mt. Borah

Yellowstone National Park

WYOMING

Caldwell

BOISE

Nampa

Arrowrock Dam

Anderson Dam

Craters of the Moon Nat. Mon.

Plains

Idaho Falls

OREGON

Snake River

Silver City

Snake

River

Alameda

Rupert

Pocatello

Shoshone Falls

American Falls Dam

Soda Springs

Twin Falls

Burley

Owyhee Plateau

Western Shoshone Ind. Res.

Shoshone Ice Caves

Ft. Hall

UTAH

NEVADA

Chief Joseph
Leader of the Nez Percés Indians in the war of 1877

William E. Borah
U.S. Senator, 1907-1940

IDAHO
Area: 83,557 square miles
Population: 667,191
Admission Date: July 3, 1890

Capital: Boise
Rank: 13th
Rank: 42nd
Rank: 43rd

Major Sources of Income:

Agriculture and Livestock
beef cattle, wheat and hay, potatoes

Manufacturing
food products, lumber and wood products, chemicals and chemical products

Lumbering

Minerals
silver, lead, zinc

Climate:
Idaho's mountains shelter the land from Canadian cold waves. In the valleys, the climate is relatively mild because warm air from the Pacific is held between the Pacific slope and Idaho's Rockies. But most of the moisture carried by the warm Pacific air is dropped before it comes over the western mountains so that Idaho's climate is not uncomfortably humid. Only the high mountain tops of the panhandle are subjected to severe weather and plentiful rain because of their exposed positions. The Plains area further south receives about one third as much rain.

Idaho's northern border is Canada. Down from Canada come the rugged northern ranges of the Rocky Mountains which cover most of Idaho. Idaho's Bitterroot Mountains are part of the Northern Rockies.

In the mountains grow the forests which cover more area than the forests of any other Rocky Mountain state. And from these mountains comes the water that irrigates Idaho's land. Only two states in the whole country have more irrigated land acres than does Idaho.

Important Whens and Whats in the Making of Idaho

1805 Lewis and Clark, during their expedition to the Pacific Coast, are the first white men to enter Idaho.

1810 The Missouri Fur Trade Company opens Fort Henry to trade with the Shoshones.

1848 Idaho is included in the Oregon Territory.

1860 Gold is discovered in Orofino Creek, and the first permanent settlement is made at Franklin.

1861 Idaho's first city, Lewiston, is built by Mormons.

1863 Idaho, including Montana and parts of Wyoming, Nebraska and the Dakotas, becomes a Territory.

1877 Chief Joseph is defeated in the Nez Percés War.

1880-1884 Railroad lines begin to cross Idaho.

1884 Coeur d'Alene is found to be one of the world's richest silver, lead and zinc districts.

1890 Idaho is admitted to the Union as the 43rd State.

67

The Snake River Plains, part of the Columbia Plateau, reach across Idaho's central section. The Snake River cuts across the lava-flow plains to drain into the Pacific-bound Columbia River. On this journey for thousands of years, the Snake cut Hell's Canyon almost 2,000 feet deeper than the Grand Canyon and made it the deepest on the North American continent.

Idaho's southern section is a bit of Basin and Range area which, in Utah, becomes the land of the Great Salt Lake and the Great Basin.

In Idaho's panhandle are mountain wilderness areas, some that have barely been explored. Here there are hundreds of small lakes carved out by wind, water and glacial action, as well as Idaho's three largest lakes, Priest, Pend Oreille and Coeur d'Alene.

Hunting and fishing is good in Idaho. More than half of Idaho's people have hunting and fishing licenses. Sun Valley is a famous spot for skiing and other winter sports. Idaho has Shoshone Falls—higher than Niagara—Lava Hot Springs, Craters of the Moon and Shoshone Ice Caves.

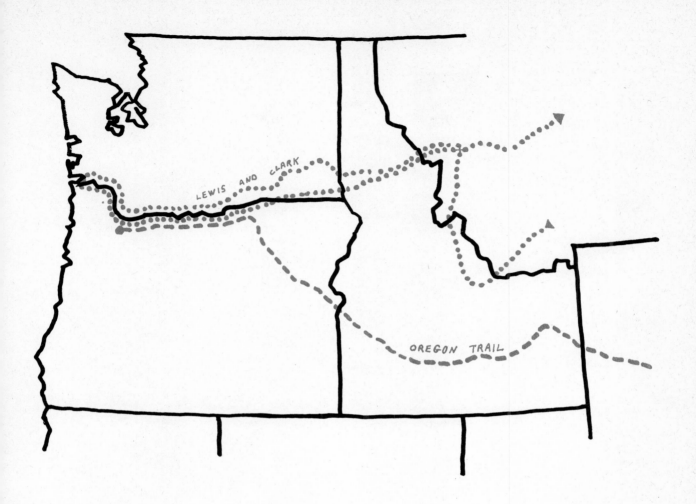

The old Oregon Trail and the route that Lewis and Clark traveled on their way to the Pacific Ocean wind through Idaho.

Idaho's people are farmers, lumbermen, miners, ranchers, machinery manufacturers, atomic energy scientists and food and goods processors.

Idaho is a land of contrasts—old and new, hot and cold, high and low. Mount Borah's peak hits the 12,655 foot mark. Lewiston is the low mark at 738 feet where the Snake swings west out of the state. There are old mining towns whose days are all but ended and nuclear reactor testing stations, part of the United States Atomic Energy Research Laboratories, whose days have only just begun.

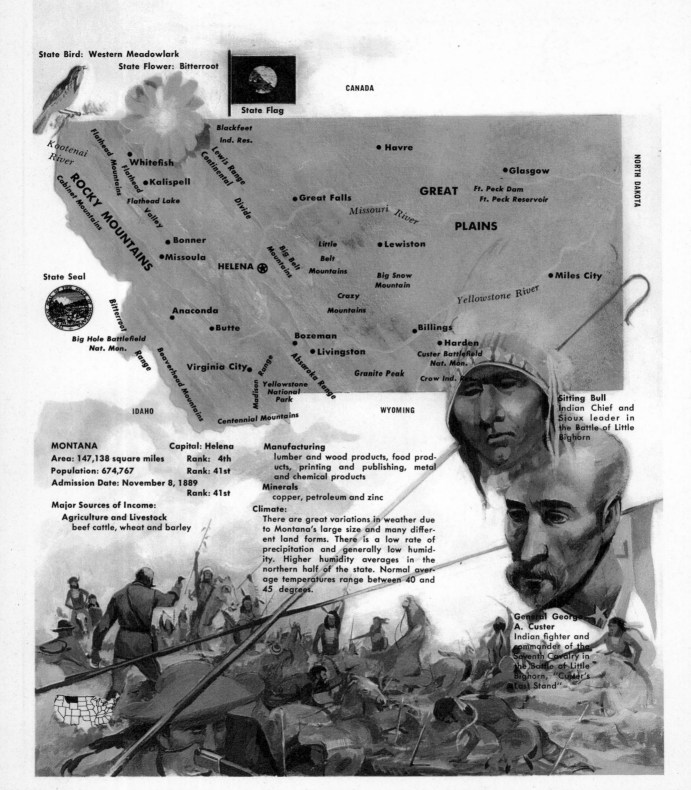

State Bird: Western Meadowlark
State Flower: Bitterroot

State Flag

CANADA

Kootenai River

Blackfeet
Ind. Res.

• Havre

• Glasgow

GREAT

Ft. Peck Dam
Ft. Peck Reservoir

ROCKY MOUNTAINS

Flathead Mountains
Cabinet Mountains

• Whitefish

• Kalispell

Flathead
Valley

Flathead Lake

Lewis Range

Continental Divide

• Great Falls

Missouri River

PLAINS

• Bonner

• Missoula

Big Belt Mountains

Little
Belt
Mountains

• Lewiston

Big Snow
Mountain

• Miles City

HELENA ✪

Crazy
Mountains

Yellowstone River

State Seal

Bitterroot Range

• Anaconda

• Butte

Bozeman •

• Billings

• Harden

Big Hole Battlefield
Nat. Mon.

Beaverhead Mountains

• Livingston

Custer Battlefield
Nat. Mon.

Virginia City •

Madison Range

Absaroka Range

Granite Peak

Crow Ind. Res.

Yellowstone
National
Park

IDAHO

Centennial Mountains

WYOMING

NORTH DAKOTA

Sitting Bull
Indian Chief and
Sioux leader in
the Battle of Little
Bighorn

MONTANA

Area: 147,138 square miles
Population: 674,767
Admission Date: November 8, 1889

Capital: Helena
Rank: 4th
Rank: 41st

Rank: 41st

Major Sources of Income:
Agriculture and Livestock
beef cattle, wheat and barley

Manufacturing
lumber and wood products, food products, printing and publishing, metal
and chemical products

Minerals
copper, petroleum and zinc

Climate:
There are great variations in weather due
to Montana's large size and many different land forms. There is a low rate of
precipitation and generally low humidity. Higher humidity averages in the
northern half of the state. Normal average temperatures range between 40 and
45 degrees.

**General George
A. Custer**
Indian fighter and
commander of the
Seventh Cavalry in
the Battle of Little
Bighorn, "Custer's
Last Stand"

Montana, in Latin, means mountainous. When the early French trappers first saw the Big Horns, they wrote of them as the "shining mountains." Also within Montana's borders are the mountains of Glacier and Yellowstone National Parks. Granite Peak at 12,850 feet, near Cooke City, is the highest point in the state.

In 1841, almost fifty years before Montana became a state, Father Pierre Jean de Smet built Montana's first church, St. Mary's Mission, in the western section of the state, the land of deep pine forests, glacier lakes and waterfalls. Flathead Lake is the largest fresh-water lake west of the Mississippi River. Here in Montana's rugged highlands are the deep copper mines of Butte. Mining and lumbering are the chief industries of this area. Near the headwaters of the Missouri, where the Lewis and Clark expedition started over the mountains, Montana's Lewis and Clark Caverns glitter with stalactite and stalagmite formations.

Important Whens and Whats in the Making of Montana

1743 French fur trappers, the Vérendryes, are probably the first white men to tell of the "Land of the Shining Mountains."

1805 Lewis and Clark make the first extensive exploration.

1807 American fur traders make the first permanent settlement at Big Horn River.

1864 Montana becomes a Territory. Gold strike at Last Chance Gulch.

1876 General Custer makes his "Last Stand" in the Battle of the Little Bighorn.

1877 After the Battle of Big Hole, Chief Joseph starts the retreat of the Indians that will end the Nez Percés War.

1889 Montana is admitted to the Union as the 41st State.

1890s "Copper barons" fight for wealth and power at Butte and in the state legislature.

The huge Fort Peck Dam across the Missouri is the largest earth-fill dam in the world. Here are the flat eastern prairies and tablelands of cattle ranches, and the wheat farms that rank Montana third in national wheat production. Near Hardin is the site of the Battle of the Little-Bighorn, Custer's Last Stand, of 1876.

Last Chance Gulch, the scene of gold strikes in Montana's frontier history, still shows off a bit of the Old West. Right in the midst of Montana's busy capitol, Helena, it still contains the history and sights of by-gone days.

Flour mills grind Montana wheat into premium flour. Sugar beet factories process beets into sugar. Canneries preserve Montana cherries, peas, beans and apples for the nation. Copper and lead, processed and refined in Montana mills, become primary metals and copper wire. Ponderosa pine, lodgepole pine, western larch, fir and spruce from Montana's mountain forests go into building materials, wood and paper products and Christmas trees.

Not only do bull moose and grizzly bear roam Montana mountains, but buffalo, American bison, graze on Montana's National Bison Range.

A Canadian border state, Montana is a land of modern cities, huge wheat and cattle ranges, farming communities, dude ranches, modern-day mining camps, Indian reservations and remote wilderness areas, almost unknown to man.

ASSAY OFFICE

State Seal

State Bird: Mountain Bluebird

OREGON

IDAHO

State Flower: Sagebrush

State Flag

Humboldt River

Winnemucca

Rye Patch Reservoir

● Elko

Beowawe Geyser Field

Black Rock Desert

● Lovelock

GREAT

Diamond Mountains

Ruby Mountains

UTAH

Pyramid Lake

Stillwater Range

Reno ●

● Austin

Shoshone Range

Virginia City

● Eureka

● McGill

River

Toiyabe Range

Ruth ●

⊛ **CARSON CITY**

Carson

Hot Creek Mountains

● Ely

Mt. Wheeler

Lake Tahoe

Walker Lake

● Gabbs

Pancake Range

Lehman Caves
Nat. Mon.

● Hawthorne

BASIN

Cathedral Gorge

● Tonopah

● Caliente

CALIFORNIA

Boundary Peak

● Goldfield

*Death Valley
Nat. Mon.*

Lake Mead

Las Vegas ●

● Hoover Dam

Boulder City ●

ARIZONA

Colorado River

CALIFORNIA

NEVADA

Capital: Carson City

Area: 110,540 square miles   Rank: 7th

Population: 285,278   Rank: 49th

Admission Date: October 31, 1864   Rank: 36th

Major Sources of Income:

Minerals
   manganese, copper

Agriculture and Livestock
   beef cattle, hay and wheat

Manufacturing
   stone, clay and glass products, food products

Climate:
Nevada is mostly dry with abundant sunshine, moderate seasonal temperatures and light rainfall. The southeast section of the state is very dry. Average annual temperatures range from desert-dry 60-65 degrees near Las Vegas to 40-45 degrees in the northern parts.

Kit Carson
Famous frontiersman and guide for Frémont's early explorations of Nevada.

John C. Frémont
The first man to accurately map the Nevada Territory

Most of Nevada is dry barren desert country lying in the Great Basin area between the Sierra Nevadas, and the Great Salt Lake and Desert region of Utah.

More than twenty mountain ranges cross the state, separated by long desert valleys. Nevada's high points, Boundary Peak and Wheeler Peak, measure over 13,000 feet. The low spot of the state lies along the Colorado River in Nevada's southern border point, not quite 500 feet above sea level. There are few rivers in the greater part of Nevada, which lies within the Great Basin region, and none finds outlet to the sea.

With its deserts, mountains, and its limited supply of water, it is easy to understand why Nevada was no haven for early settlers and continues to be the least populous state except for Alaska.

Important Whens and Whats in the Making of Nevada

1775 Spanish explorer-missionary Francisco Tomás Garcés and his expedition are probably the first white men to enter the Nevada region.

1843-1845 Captain John C. Frémont's expedition, guided by Kit Carson, explores the Nevada territory.

1848 The Nevada region is included in the land ceded to the United States at the end of the Mexican War.

1849 Nevada's first permanent settlement is made at Genoa on the Carson River.

1850 Nevada becomes part of the Utah Territory by the Compromise of 1850.

1859 Discovery of Virginia City's Comstock Lode, one of the richest deposits of gold and silver ever found.

1861 Congress creates the Nevada Territory.

1864 Nevada, the first state of the High Country to become one of the United States, is admitted to the Union as the 36th State.

But California was on the other side of Nevada's Sierra Nevada
Mountains. During the California gold rush, covered wagons stopped
for supplies at Nevada's first town, Mormon Station, before crossing
the mountains to California. Then Las Vegas began in 1855 as a
Mormon fort. Soon pony express and Overland Mail riders traveled
across Nevada's mountain and desert lands.

Settlers came to stay in Nevada when gold and silver were discovered in 1859 at Virginia City. More deposits were opened in Austin,
Eureka, Tonopah and Goldfield. Mining is still important to Nevada.
The state produces almost half of the nation's manganese and more
tungsten than any other state. One of the world's largest open-pit
copper mines is near Ely.

When the Central Pacific Railroad was completed in Nevada in 1868, new towns were built and soon became shipping centers for ranch and farm products. Nevada's open ranges in the eastern sections are grazing lands for cattle, sheep, hogs and horses. Ranching is the most important phase of industry in Nevada since there is proportionately less land used for farming here than in any other state.

Hoover Dam, on the Colorado River between Arizona and Nevada, forms Lake Mead. Lake Tahoe is on the mountain border of the Sierras between California and Nevada. These two lakes are famous Nevada recreation spots.

Within its barren, rugged borders, Nevada has geysers—Beowawe Geyser Field, second only to Yellowstone's exhibit, ghost towns—Rhyolite, near Death Valley, and Hamilton in the east, and gambling casinos in Reno and Las Vegas that are advertised on highway billboards far from this Rocky Mountain state.

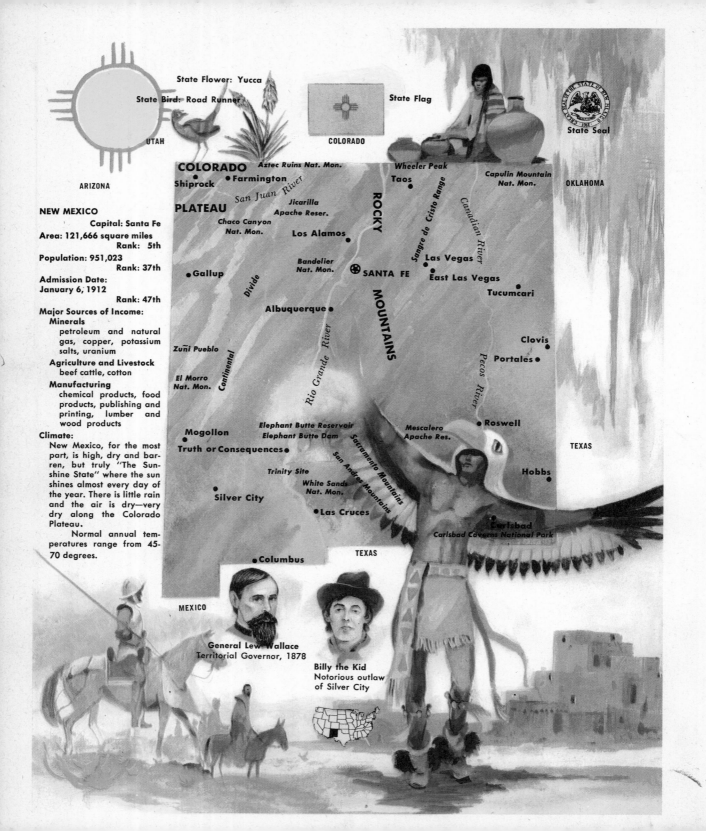

State Flower: Yucca

State Bird: Road Runner

State Flag

State Seal

UTAH

ARIZONA

NEW MEXICO

Capital: Santa Fe

Area: 121,666 square miles
Rank: 5th

Population: 951,023
Rank: 37th

Admission Date:
January 6, 1912
Rank: 47th

Major Sources of Income:
Minerals
petroleum and natural gas, copper, potassium salts, uranium
Agriculture and Livestock
beef cattle, cotton
Manufacturing
chemical products, food products, publishing and printing, lumber and wood products

Climate:
New Mexico, for the most part, is high, dry and barren, but truly "The Sunshine State" where the sun shines almost every day of the year. There is little rain and the air is dry—very dry along the Colorado Plateau.
Normal annual temperatures range from 45-70 degrees.

COLORADO

Aztec Ruins Nat. Mon.

Wheeler Peak

Taos

Capulin Mountain Nat. Mon.

OKLAHOMA

Shiprock • Farmington

San Juan River

PLATEAU

Jicarilla Apache Reser.

ROCKY

Sangre de Cristo Range

Canadian River

Chaco Canyon Nat. Mon.

Los Alamos

• Gallup

Bandelier Nat. Mon.

SANTA FE

Las Vegas

East Las Vegas

Tucumcari

MOUNTAINS

Albuquerque •

Continental

Divide

Zuñi Pueblo

Rio Grande River

Pecos River

Clovis

Portales •

El Morro Nat. Mon.

Elephant Butte Reservoir
Elephant Butte Dam

Mescalero Apache Res.

Roswell

TEXAS

Mogollon •
Truth or Consequences •

Sacramento Mountains

Hobbs •

Trinity Site

San Andres Mountains

White Sands Nat. Mon.

• Silver City

Carlsbad
Carlsbad Caverns National Park

• Las Cruces

• Columbus

TEXAS

MEXICO

General Lew Wallace
Territorial Governor, 1878

Billy the Kid
Notorious outlaw of Silver City

Two ranges of the Rocky Mountains stretch down into New Mexico. Between them lies the Rio Grande Valley where the Rio Grande runs through on its way down to the Gulf of Mexico. The early Spanish explorers came through this valley following the river and its western forks. These first white men to enter the High Country followed the rivers to the old Indian pueblos and ancient ruins.

The Spanish were looking for gold. More than 400 years later, the search is for uranium. New Mexico's cliffs and canyons contain more than 70 per cent of our country's known uranium resources.

Important Whens and Whats in the Making of New Mexico

1536   Alvar Núñez Cabeza de Vaca brings stories of "Seven Golden Cities" back to Mexico after probably being the first white man to enter what is now New Mexico.

1540-1542   Francisco Vásquez de Coronado undertakes early exploration.

1598   The Spanish, under Juan de Oñate, make the first settlement at San Juan de los Caballeros.

1680-1692   The Pueblo Uprising destroys Spanish settlements.

1692   Spanish dominance re-established by Don Diego de Vargas.

1821   The region of New Mexico comes under Mexican rule after Mexico's revolt from Spain.

1846   General Stephen W. Kearny takes possession of New Mexico for the United States after a bloodless conquest.

1848   After the Mexican War, the land of New Mexico is annexed to the United States.

1886   Surrender of the Apaches ends Indian warfare.

1912   New Mexico is admitted to the Union as the 47th State.

Pueblo, Navajo, and Apache Indians live in New Mexico today. Their homes are small villages founded before the Spanish came, scattered hogans, or farms on tribal lands set aside by the government. Today lumbering, leases from oil and gas and uranium deposits, stock raising, and farming enterprises are income sources for tribes that once were silversmiths, weavers, and pottery makers.

Founded 1609–1610, New Mexico's capital city of Santa Fe is now a modern busy place where shadows of the past are ever-present. In this city is the Palace of the Governors where the Spanish rulers had their offices. The Palace, now the major unit of the State Museum of New Mexico, was the first public building in America.

Throughout the state the past rubs shoulders with the present and future. New Mexico is a land of mountains and deserts and ice caves and the great Carlsbad Caverns, there before the time of man. There are many ruins of ancient Indian pueblos, and there are Indian villages that are still occupied by the descendants of the people who lived here before the white men came to the High Country. Old military outposts and forts are signposts of New Mexico's pioneer past.

Pancho Villa's men, and perhaps even the notorious Mexican bandit-hero himself, came over the border to New Mexico in 1916 and staged a raid in Columbus. New Mexico is the last resting place of the infamous American outlaw, Billy the Kid.

Elephant Butte Dam on the Rio Grande and the Conchas Dam on the Canadian River are New Mexico progress points of today. Trinity Site marks the spot of America's first atomic bomb explosion.

National forests, Indian reservations, mesas, mountains and caves, today and yesterday are all a part of New Mexico.

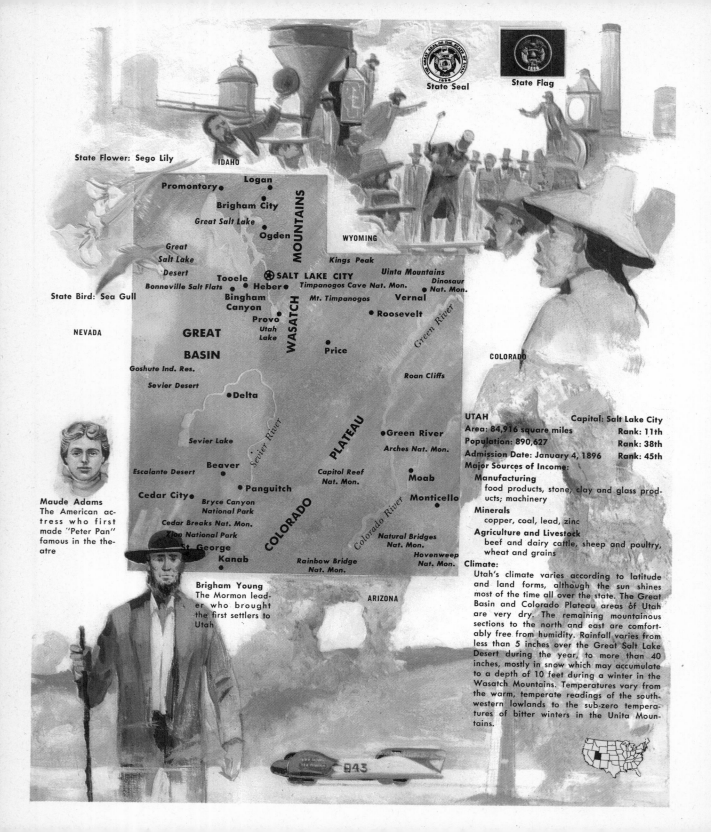

State Seal

State Flag

State Flower: Sego Lily

State Bird: Sea Gull

IDAHO

Promontory
Logan
Brigham City
Great Salt Lake
Ogden

WYOMING

MOUNTAINS

Great
Salt Lake
Desert

Tooele
Heber
Bonneville Salt Flats
Bingham
Canyon

Kings Peak

Uinta Mountains
Timpanogos Cave Nat. Mon.
Dinosaur
Nat. Mon.

SALT LAKE CITY

WASATCH

Mt. Timpanogos

Vernal

NEVADA

GREAT

BASIN

Provo
Utah
Lake

Roosevelt

Price

Green River

COLORADO

Goshute Ind. Res.

Sevier Desert

Delta

Roan Cliffs

Sevier Lake

Sevier River

Green River
Arches Nat. Mon.

Maude Adams
The American actress who first made "Peter Pan" famous in the theatre

Escalante Desert

Beaver

Cedar City

Panguitch

Bryce Canyon
National Park

Cedar Breaks Nat. Mon.

Zion National Park

St. George

Kanab

PLATEAU

COLORADO

Capitol Reef
Nat. Mon.

Moab

Monticello

Colorado River

Natural Bridges
Nat. Mon.

Rainbow Bridge
Nat. Mon.

Hovenweep
Nat. Mon.

Brigham Young
The Mormon leader who brought the first settlers to Utah

ARIZONA

UTAH   Capital: Salt Lake City
Area: 84,916 square miles   Rank: 11th
Population: 890,627   Rank: 38th
Admission Date: January 4, 1896   Rank: 45th

Major Sources of Income:

Manufacturing
food products, stone, clay and glass products; machinery

Minerals
copper, coal, lead, zinc

Agriculture and Livestock
beef and dairy cattle, sheep and poultry, wheat and grains

Climate:
Utah's climate varies according to latitude and land forms, although the sun shines most of the time all over the state. The Great Basin and Colorado Plateau areas of Utah are very dry. The remaining mountainous sections to the north and east are comfortably free from humidity. Rainfall varies from less than 5 inches over the Great Salt Lake Desert during the year, to more than 40 inches, mostly in snow which may accumulate to a depth of 10 feet during a winter in the Wasatch Mountains. Temperatures vary from the warm, temperate readings of the southwestern lowlands to the sub-zero temperatures of bitter winters in the Unita Mountains.

843

Utah is a land of many lands. The state's share of Rocky Mountain region includes green valleys lying in the shadow of the Wasatch Mountains, and the wilderness areas of water and timberlands of the Uinta Range. Here are Utah's highest peaks and the geologic curiosities and ancient relics of Dinosaur National Monument.

Utah's portion of the Colorado Plateau is a colorful land of high plateaus and deserts cut by the Colorado and Green rivers. Rolling dry valleys and strange white deserts make up Utah's Basin and Range province of the Great Basin.

Ute, Paiute and Shoshoni Indians were Utah residents long before the Spanish missionary-explorers made their trip across the Green River. This was the site of the Crossing of the Fathers late in the 1700s, more than fifty years before Utah's first trading post, Fort Roubidoux, was built.

Important Whens and Whats in the Making of Utah

1776 Spanish missionaries, Escalante and Domínguez, are the first white men to explore Utah.

1831-1846 Mexican trading expeditions from Santa Fe bring caravans through Utah to California on the "Spanish Trail."

1837 Antoine Roubidoux builds a fur trading post, Fort Roubidoux.

1847 The Mormons build a town at Salt Lake.

1848 The Utah region becomes the property of the United States after the Mexican War.

1849 The temporary State of Deseret is formed by the Mormons.

1850 The Utah Territory is created by Congress. Brigham Young is the first Territorial Governor.

1869 The first transcontinental railroad in America is finished with a golden spike at Promontory.

1896 Utah is admitted to the Union as the 45th State.

Early immigrant wagon and mule trains rolled around and across the Great Salt Desert on their way to California in the 1830s and 1840s. The Mormons started Utah's first real settlement around the Great Salt Lake.

The 2,000 square mile salt lake that has no outlet to the sea was first explored in 1825 by James Bridger. Now a railroad bridge carries passenger trains over the lake's seventy-five mile length. Salt is taken from the lake for commercial uses. The vast salt wastelands to the west, Bonneville Salt Flats, are the scene of automobile races and automotive endurance tests.

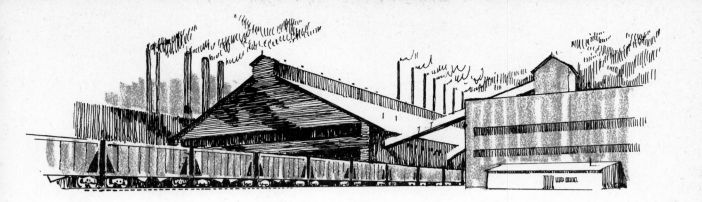

In the early 1900s, Utah's open-cut mining operations and smelters made the state the largest non-ferrous smelting center in the world. Coal fields came into production. The production of sugar from beets became an important industry.

In recent years, oil and uranium industries, manufacturing concerns, and military installations have come to Utah.

Some of Utah's natural resources are protected in national forests. Reseeding and reforestation programs, the control of grazing and improved farming methods, and the building of dams, reservoirs and canals promote the wise use of Utah's other natural assets.

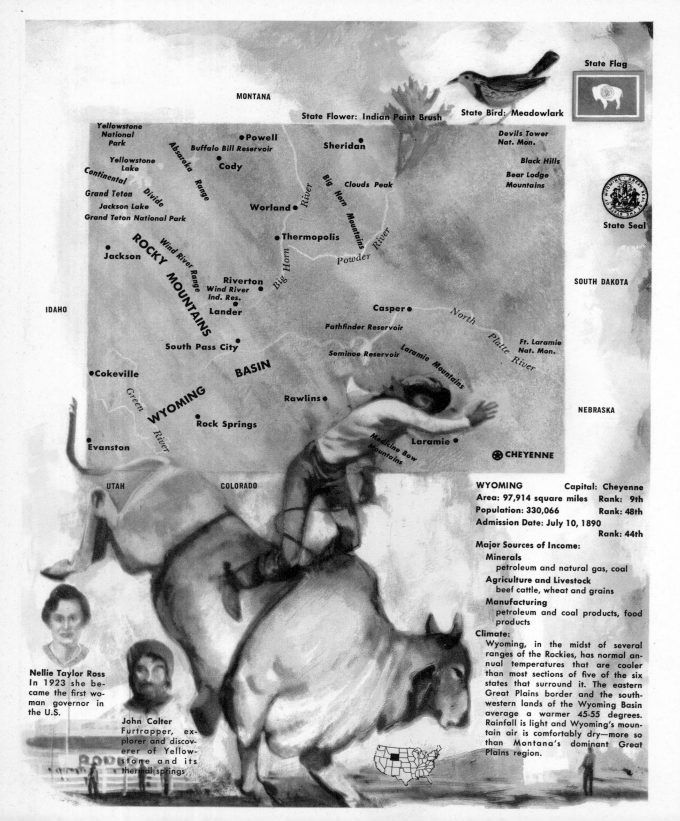

MONTANA

State Flower: Indian Paint Brush

State Bird: Meadowlark

State Flag

Yellowstone
National
Park

Powell

Buffalo Bill Reservoir

Sheridan

Devils Tower
Nat. Mon.

Yellowstone
Lake

Absaroka Range

Cody

Black Hills

Bear Lodge
Mountains

Continental

Big Horn River

Clouds Peak

Grand Teton

Divide

Worland

Jackson Lake

Big Horn Mountains

Grand Teton National Park

Thermopolis

Powder River

State Seal

ROCKY

Wind River Range

Jackson

MOUNTAINS

Riverton
Wind River
Ind. Res.

SOUTH DAKOTA

Lander

Casper

North Platte River

South Pass City

Pathfinder Reservoir

Ft. Laramie
Nat. Mon.

Seminoe Reservoir

Laramie Mountains

Cokeville

WYOMING

BASIN

NEBRASKA

Rawlins

Green River

Rock Springs

Medicine Bow Mountains

Laramie

Evanston

CHEYENNE

UTAH

COLORADO

IDAHO

Nellie Taylor Ross
In 1923 she be-
came the first wo-
man governor in
the U.S.

John Colter
Furtrapper, ex-
plorer and discov-
erer of Yellow-
stone and its
thermal springs

WYOMING   Capital: Cheyenne
Area: 97,914 square miles   Rank: 9th
Population: 330,066   Rank: 48th
Admission Date: July 10, 1890
                            Rank: 44th

Major Sources of Income:
  Minerals
    petroleum and natural gas, coal
  Agriculture and Livestock
    beef cattle, wheat and grains
  Manufacturing
    petroleum and coal products, food
    products

Climate:
  Wyoming, in the midst of several
  ranges of the Rockies, has normal annual temperatures that are cooler
  than most sections of five of the six
  states that surround it. The eastern
  Great Plains border and the southwestern lands of the Wyoming Basin
  average a warmer 45-55 degrees.
  Rainfall is light and Wyoming's mountain air is comfortably dry—more so
  than Montana's dominant Great
  Plains region.

Wyoming is a state of vast forests, towering mountains, sweeping plains and more than 5,000 lakes. Much of Wyoming is made up of plains which stretch almost as far as you can see. But mighty mountain ranges tower to heights of nearly 14,000 feet.

The mountains of the Snowy Range with the Medicine Bow National Forest are in the southeast, while the Big Horns and the Absarokas cross the northern border. Vast wilderness areas are in the west-central Wind River Range and further west lies the Swiss-like region of Star Valley and the majestic Tetons.

Important Whens and Whats in the Making of Wyoming

1743	French fur trappers, the Vérendryes, are probably the first white men to enter Wyoming lands.
1811-1812	Fur trading expeditions come to Wyoming.
1834	Americans build a trading post, Fort Laramie.
1860-1870	Indian warfare does not stop the flow of new residents.
1869	Esther Hobart Morris gives a tea party in South Pass City which is to result in the right to vote for women.
1890	Wyoming is admitted to the Union as the 44th State.
1910	Oil boom in Wyoming.

The mountains of Wyoming contain great coal reserves. Mineral waters lie under the land. The world's largest hot springs are located in Thermopolis.

Immigrant wagon trains, the pony express and herds of Texas longhorns came to Wyoming in the old days. Fort Laramie and Fort Bridger were important frontier cavalry posts along the Oregon, California and Mormon trails during the days of the Indian Wars. They also served as relay points for the pony express.

Rodeos, pageants and celebrations such as Cheyenne Frontier Days, Sheridan's All-American Indian Days and the Gift of the Waters pageant at Thermopolis tell stories of frontier Wyoming.

Buffalo Bill's hunting lodge and Wild West Museum can be seen in Cody, the city founded by the hunter and Indian scout, a legend in song and story.

Independence Rock, southwest of Casper, bears the names and initials of hundreds of the people who passed that way in covered wagons heading west. Many of these early travelers who came by way of the old Oregon Trail passed through South Pass City. Snuggled in a gulch below the Continental Divide, South Pass City, now a Wyoming ghost town, was once a thriving city.

Grateful acknowledgment is made to the following for the helpful information and materials furnished by them, used in the preparation of this book:

United States Department of the Interior, National Park Service; particularly, the National Parks of: Bryce Canyon, Carlsbad Caverns, Glacier, Grand Canyon, Grand Teton, Mesa Verde, Rocky Mountain, Yellowstone, Zion; and their respective managements.

United States Department of Commerce, Bureau of the Census, Field Services, Chicago, Illinois.

State of Arizona Development Board.

State of Colorado Advertising and Publicity Department.

State of Idaho Department of Commerce and Development.

Montana Chamber of Commerce.

The Historical Society of Montana.

Montana State Advertising Department.

New Mexico Department of Development.

State of Nevada Department of Economic Development.

Utah Tourist and Publicity Council.

Wyoming Travel Commission.

International Visual Educational Services, Inc., Chicago, Illinois.

Glossary

adobe (*à* dō′bǐ) 1. sun dried, unburnt, brick used for building purposes; 2. a type of Indian dwelling.

aerodynamics (ā′ēr ô dī năm′ǐks) the study of the motion of air and other gases and forces acting on bodies in motion (through air).

aqueduct (ăk′wē dŭkt) 1. a channel for flowing water; 2. a structure for carrying water over a river or hollow.

archaeologist (är′kē ŏl′ô jǐst) a specialist in the study of the remains of past human life, such as fossil relics, monuments, etc.

bulldogging (bŏŏl′dôg ǐng) throwing a steer by seizing its horns and twisting its neck.

chasm (kăz′m) a deep gap or opening, as in the earth.

culture (kŭl′tŭr) 1. a particular stage in the development of a civilization; 2. the characteristic features of such a stage.

cyclotron (sī′klô trŏn) an apparatus used to bombard the center of atoms to produce changes and artificial radioactivity.

dry farming (drī fär′mǐng) the production of crops without irrigation in regions of little rainfall, chiefly by conserving soil moisture and raising crops requiring little moisture.

91

mesa (mā′sả) a flat-topped rocky hill with steeply sloping sides.

narrow gauge tracks (năr′ō gāj trăks) tracks smaller than standard railroad tracks, usually used in mines.

non-ferrous (nŏn - fĕr′ŭs) having no iron; including metals other than iron.

nuclear reactor (nū′klể ĕr rể ăk′tẽr) the center of an atomic mass or substance which responds to certain chemical treatments.

earth-fill dam (ûrth - fĭl dăm) a restraining barrier of earth for the purpose of stopping the flow of water.

eruption (ể rŭp′shŭn) the act of breaking out or bursting forth, especially of confined elements within the earth.

fissure (fĭsh′ẽr) a narrow opening, a crack, or a split.

geyser (gī′zẽr; gī′sẽr) a spring which throws forth periodic jets of heated water and steam.

Gila monster (hē′lả mŏn′stẽr) a large orange-and-black poisonous lizard.

grandeur (grăn′dụ̆r) grandness, magnificence, splendor, greatness.

greenhorn (grēn′hôrn′) a raw, inexperienced person.

grouse (grous) a plump, strong bird with feathered legs and a plume, usually spotted with red-brown or other colors which help to conceal it.

helictite (hể lĭk′tīt) a curious twisted form of stalactite; spiral shape is the result of cavern air currents. (see stalactite)

kiva (kē′vả) an Indian ceremonial chamber.

mammoth (măm′ŭth) a large elephant no longer living.

manganese (măng′gả nēs) a grayish-white metal with reddish tinge, harder than iron, not magnetic; used in steel to increase its hardness.

open-pit mine (ōpĕn - pĭt mīn) a mine in an opening of the earth's surface; not covered.

parasite (păr′a sīt) one who lives off of someone else.

petroglyph (pĕt′rŏ glĭf) a carving upon a rock, especially a prehistoric one.

phenomena (fĕ nŏm′ĕ na) rare or very unusual facts or events.

pinnacle (pĭn′a k′l) a tall, slender, pointed mass, especially a lofty peak.

pit house (pĭt hous) a large hole or depression, used by prehistoric man as a dwelling place or shelter.

pueblo (pwĕb′lō) an Indian village built of stone or adobe in the form of continuously joined houses.

road runner (rōd rŭn′ĕr) a bird of the cockoo family, noted for running with great speed.

semi-arid (sĕm′ĭ - ăr′ĭd) partially dry; with little moisture.

stalactite (sta lăk′tīt) a deposit of calcium carbonate, resembling an icicle, hanging from the roof or sides of a cavern. It is formed by the continuous dripping of water mixed with calcium carbonate. As the moisture evaporates a deposit is left which forms the downward peak.

stalagmite (sta lăg′mīt) a deposit of calcium carbonate formed on the floor of a cavern as a result of the continuous formation of a stalactite. This column builds up as the deposited calcium carbonate is left after evaporation.

tableland (tā′b′l lănd) a broad elevated plateau with steep cliff-like sides leading down to the adjoining lowlands or sea.

tuff (tŭf) a rock consisting of volcanic ash which has been thrown out by a volcano during eruption.

tungsten (tŭng′stĕn) a metallic natural resource, white in color, mined for use in electric lights and steel refining.